Congratulations on Your Divorce

Congratulations On Your *Divorce*

THE ROAD TO FINDING YOUR HAPPILY EVER AFTER

Amy Botwinick

Health Communications, Inc.
Deerfield Beach, Florida

www.hcibooks.com

While this book is intended to be a catapult for positive change, it is not meant to replace the advice of legal, financial or medical professionals.

Library of Congress Cataloging-in-Publication Data
is available from the Library of Congress.

©2005 Amy Botwinick
ISBN 0-7573-0322-6

Publisher: Health Communications, Inc.
3201 S.W. 15th Street
Deerfield Beach, FL 33442-8190

Author photo by David Eric
Cover design by Andrea Perrine Brower
Inside book design by Dawn Von Strolley Grove

Contents

Acknowledgments

First I want to thank the many brave women and men who agreed to let me interview them for this book. They generously offered advice, hope and laughter that helped me through my own journey as I put many of their words on paper. I want to thank my editor, Elisabeth Rinaldi, for keeping me on track and Dr. David Lubetkin for his knowledge and mission to keep women healthy.

To my parents, Linda and Allan, thank you for being a constant source of love and support and having the energy to put up with me day or night. My sister, for laughing and crying with me, and my beautiful boys whose smiling faces remind me to laugh and enjoy the ride. Gary, for teaching me about love, friendship and getting it right—even when I get it wrong—and his wonderful kids for letting me into their lives.

I want to thank my friends: Susan for always listening and having a great contact; Donna, for her openness and honesty; Jill, for never sugar-coating her edits; Kelly, for being my legal guardian angel; Don and Carolyn, for being my go-to couple for unwavering support; Jodi and Stacey, for always standing by me since we were kids; and my dear friend, Susan, from across the pond, who was always there regardless of the distance. For everyone else not mentioned (you know who you are) the greatest gifts I have been given are your friendship and love. Thank you.

Part One

The Journey

(jer ne) n. the act of going from one place to another

Chapter

1

Reality Check

Prince Charming has either turned into a toad
or run off with Sleeping Beauty; now what?!

"Now what?" turns out to be the ultimate question when a woman starts to look at divorce head-on. As I fumbled my way through the process I felt desperate and uncertain before, during and after the divorce. I was charting unknown territory at a time when I was barely functioning as a result of my "divorce hangover." I just wanted to close my eyes and have somebody else deal with the whole mess and wake me up when it was over. Every morning I would force myself out of bed and wonder how this became my life and how I was going to make it through another day. I'm sure these feelings are all too familiar.

Regardless of where you are in your process, this book will help you get a grip. Facing yourself and the reality of your situation can be overwhelming and paralyzing. This book will give you tools to be productive and more objective in your decisions by minimizing some of the "trauma drama" that naturally accompanies divorce. This will give you clarity to break down the process and the courage to do what has to be done to get yourself back on track.

A divorce can seem like a life-consuming event. It can bring out a wide range of emotions, beliefs and controversy in yourself and your circle of friends and family. The good news is that this will eventually be just a blip on your radar screen. The uncomfortable situation you are in *will* change, and life is waiting for you to choose your path. Every woman has her own perspective and unique set of circumstances that will determine the choices she makes along her journey.

When my divorce became public knowledge, I was bombarded with inappropriate questions from many female acquaintances. While I was put off by their intrusiveness, I realized some of them were in "desperate housewife mode" and needed help and someone to talk to. Others were just rudely curious to see if my grass was actually greener on the other side as they contemplated and compared their own happiness.

A Good Look in the Mirror

Before moving on with what you need to know about divorce, the next few pages will ask you to *look before you leap* if you find yourself wanting out of your marriage. Because you may be the initiator of the divorce, I urge you to explore this part of the book with honesty. Choosing to divorce might ultimately be your decision, but it should be one made in a state of calm with little doubt and few regrets.

When someone approaches me and says he or she wants a divorce, my first reaction is to ask, "Are you sure?" Decisions made in haste can take on lives of their own, and before you know it, there may be no turning back to save your marriage. Deep down we all know when we are at peace with the decisions we've made—big and small. Sometimes we listen to our gut, and sometimes we don't. When we make decisions and take action while our doubt mechanism is in full gear, we know we will eventually pay for it. To avoid this scenario, respect the little voice inside you if it says "wait." Your gut instinct is asking you to reevaluate the situation before making your decision. Before making this significant change in your life, take a good look at yourself and your concept of marriage.

When you're looking at the choice to divorce, forget all about the idea of the romantic fairy tale. It's time to take a good look at marriage and understand what it really takes to make this type of partnership work. Depending on how realistic and honest you are when evaluating your situation, when it comes to a divorce, you may find that the grass is not always greener on the other side. For a good dose of reality, sit down and write out a pro and con list of staying married versus the realities of divorce and being single.

Consider the following: children, your career status and ability to make money, finances, lifestyle changes, cost of divorce, being single again, and the threat of sexually transmitted diseases once you're back on the dating circuit. (You may be thinking, "I never want to date again," but trust me, you will.)

Consider the following:
- Have you gone to marriage counseling?
- Have you and your spouse taken the time to talk and isolate the real problems of the marriage?
- Do you really listen to each other or just nag, complain and tune out?
- How well do you compromise and try to find time for enjoying quality time together?
- How productive or destructive are your methods of fighting?
- Do you kiss and make up without holding grudges?
- Are you teammates working toward the same goals?
- Are you both willing to work on your issues together?

Writing out the answers to these questions will help guide you in making an educated, rational decision. Divorce is difficult, but it might be your best option and worth the temporary discomfort of transitioning into a new life. The process of honest evaluation will help you experience more peace and have fewer doubts regardless of your decision.

"Mirror, mirror, on the wall, who's the most honest one of all?"

Part of your reality check of marriage starts with taking a good honest look at yourself. Do a self-audit of who you are and how you have changed since you have been married. Everyone has the right to enjoy their own pity party, but eventually it's time to get a grip and move on. Be the adult by putting an end to the blame game and take responsibility for your own issues and contributions to the deterioration of the relationship. Ask yourself the following questions:

- How is my self-esteem?
- What kind of life do I have outside of my family?
- Do I play the martyr role and take care of everyone while putting my own needs and wants on the bottom of the list?
- How would my husband describe how I have changed from the person I was before we married?
- Do I still know how to have fun?

Maria—42 years old

On my forty-second birthday I found out that my husband was having an affair with another woman; happy birthday to me. It was as though he wanted to get caught. I had always paid the bills, and he knew that I scrutinized the credit card statements every month. I noticed that in the billing cycle right before my birthday, there were quite a few purchases made at a woman's boutique. The day of my birthday I anxiously awaited my new gifts, only to be presented with a small bouquet of flowers.

The next day I asked him about his purchases. Just like that, he came clean about his affair. He even seemed relieved that his secret was out in the open. I felt like he vomited all over me and left me standing there in the mess.

Humiliated, angry and in shock, I locked myself in my bedroom and refused to talk to him. After two days I emerged from my cave and prepared for battle. I found a good attorney and pulled myself together to deal with my new reality with my husband. When I asked him why he did this to us, his response left me dazed and confused, he told me he missed me and wanted to get my attention.

I became outraged and called him every curse word I felt was appropriate. I told him he was ridiculous; we lived under the same roof, had our meals together and slept in the same bed. He said that was exactly his point. In his mind, we were nothing more than roommates. Our sex life had become routine and almost nonexistent. I stopped being his "Energizer bunny" and never seemed to have any fun time left over for him. I thought, "Yeah, that's right, I'm exhausted because I'm raising our kids and doing your laundry." It was so hard to hear, I started scanning the room for the heaviest object I could hurl at him; I wanted to inflict some serious pain. Somehow I controlled my urge, but I had to torture myself just a little more: I asked him if he loved her. He laughed as he shook his head no and told me that he loved me.

The conversation didn't make sense. I felt like I must be living on a different planet. He cheated on me, but he did it because he loves me; then he tells me he wants to go for counseling to save our marriage. My head was spinning, but my pride got the best of me so I continued on course with my new attorney. It wasn't until my mother told me to slow things down that I considered trying to work it out and agreed to go to therapy. After a few sessions together, the therapist wanted me to start therapy with her on my own. Now I thought she was nuts, he's the cheater and he's the one that needs help, not me. I'm the innocent victim.

A few weeks into our sessions after talking about my past, I started realizing just how lost, angry and out of touch I was. I married young, and within that first year I became pregnant with twins. My career as a reporter became a distant memory as the demands of raising two newborns became more than a full-time job. The years passed quickly and I settled nicely into mommyhood; my main focus was taking care of my family. It was a labor of love, but there were times I felt resentful that I never seemed to have enough time for myself. Over the years I guess I got used to the self-sacrifice, but looking back I think I lost myself.

An old friend from college came to see us for the twins' tenth birthday party. I had not seen her for several years and was anxious for her arrival. When we were alone she asked me how I was doing. I laughed, and then I suddenly started crying as I told her I didn't have time to think about it. She pressed the issue and told me that she didn't recognize the person I had become. She said I seemed sad, quiet, overwhelmed by my kids and disinterested in my husband. She missed the rebellious, outspoken, confident girl she used to know.

Who asked her anyway? It was all too much for me at the time, and I was happy when she went home. Life went on, but occasionally when I thought about her words, they cut me like a knife. I told myself that her single status gave her no right to lecture me about family matters. Looking back, I wish my defensive attitude would not have overpowered the wake-up call she was trying to give me.

Years passed, and my children were grown up and out of the house with their own lives. Suddenly, I was alone with my husband again, and it felt like we were strangers. Our marriage survived through the years but we seemed to have lost our spark. I decided that this was the natural evolution of marriage after raising children and did not give it much thought. He had his life and suddenly I had none—my life's work of raising children had come to a screeching halt.

Through my therapy, I realized I had slipped into a gradual, slow depression. I felt useless and lonely, and turned to daytime television for distraction and entertainment. I would sit and wonder how I became this boring couch potato. My husband would gently remind me that I had a college degree and that I used to *have a career and a zest for life. He was supportive but annoyed at my lack of initiative toward him or toward making changes to improve my situation. I knew he was right, but my depression made me apathetic, and the years just passed. Suddenly, here I was, struggling with my husband's infidelity.*

We're still married because therapy saved our relationship and helped me find myself again. My husband and I had to explode in order to come back together again. We seemed to become stronger in the broken places but it was difficult, and it came at a price that almost ended our marriage. We both made the choice to own up to our contributions to our issues, and we try to avoid the blame game. I don't excuse him for his actions, but I understood why it happened and I forgave him—but honestly it's difficult to forget. In the end we love each other and are committed to making it work. I started working part time again and feel like I am waking up to life again. I can feel the old Maria coming back.

Lessons Learned

- A partner who is having an affair is displaying symptoms of a bigger problem. It's very difficult for a marriage to survive the aftershocks of infidelity but it's possible and worth trying if both of you are committed and love each other.
- It's important not to lose yourself when you get married. Saying "I do" doesn't mean "I promise to take care of you and our children at the cost of who I am." Nobody likes a martyr, and it's a bad example to set for children.
- Remember that saying, "When a couple gets married, the woman wants to change the man but the man wants the woman to stay exactly the same."

- You should never stop growing as a person. If you get stuck from depression, don't let too much time go by before getting the help you need.

If, after some soul searching, you find reasons to work more on the marriage, I wish you the very best of luck. If you are in the middle of the business of divorcing, it might not be too late; many marriages are saved on the steps of the courthouse.

Biting the Bullet

I have earned my right to divorce.

I believe in marriage and the wonderful things that can come from a harmonious union. I worked hard to save my own before choosing to divorce and end a relationship that was beyond repair between two incompatible people. It was a decision I had agonized over for many difficult years. I felt like we had exhausted every possibility to make it work, and it was just time for the misery to be over for both of us.

I spoke to many women who made the decision to initiate divorce and asked them what the defining moment was that made them realize they needed to get out. Most women said it wasn't after a horrible fight or incident. They said it was a quiet moment of reflection or a simple interaction with their spouse that gave them the clarity they needed to see their big picture.

Alexis—36 years old

My defining moment came one day in an ice-cream parlor as I sat alone feeling empty inside, staring into my melting cup of butter pecan. I had just finished a two-hour conversation with my spouse, who told me he wanted to work on our marriage.

This was quite a shock because he had threatened divorce several times and completely ignored me for months. He even refused to acknowledge our ten-year anniversary.

Our marriage had been a repetitive circle—a dance of words and actions that didn't match up. I wanted to be more than just sex and a showpiece on his arm. We looked great to the outside world, but on the inside our marriage was like a hollow shell. The slightest sign of attention or minimum effort would keep me hanging on, hoping he would take a real interest in me and our marriage. He always promised things would change when we were in crisis mode, and he knew I was at the end of my rope. Once things had calmed down between us, his efforts were short-lived and the neglect would start again.

While I had my doubts, our latest conversation was different because I had finally stopped trying and it scared him. He actually said he would "jump through hoops" to win back my love and affection, and he apologized for treating me so poorly. I was almost convinced we might have a chance as I tried to forget how many times we had been through this. I decided to forget the past and live in the present. I told him I needed his friendship and some quality time alone as a couple and those things were non-negotiable. He assured me he wanted the same thing, and I was hopeful. Rather than believing this was just another attempt to keep things status quo so his life wouldn't be disrupted, I bought into the fact that he really wanted me this time.

Feeling drained and excited after talking for the last two hours, I cheerfully suggested we walk down the block to get some ice cream together. He looked at me and said he wasn't hungry. I smiled and asked if he would just come and keep me company. He looked at me as if somebody caused him physical pain as he reluctantly agreed.

Bam! That was it for me. Whether he couldn't or wouldn't

didn't matter anymore. This man didn't deliver even the simplest request like taking his wife for ice cream just to hang out together. I told him it was okay to go home and he was relieved. The funny thing was, I was relieved too because I no longer wanted to be with somebody who didn't want to be with me. I was also sad and angry because I realized I was with a guy way too long who couldn't give me some very basic things a married relationship needs to survive. I knew at that moment I finally had to leave, and that I would never eat butter pecan ice cream again.

It's funny, I felt that universal sentiment that women describe when they know a relationship is over. After putting my blood, sweat and tears into the marriage and not getting back what I needed, my well of giving finally dried up. I finally realized that there was nothing he could do to turn my heart back or change my mind. I wanted out of the marriage. It was time to end the misery. When it was crystal clear that divorce was my next step, I felt the weight on my shoulders disappear and a feeling of peace wash over me. While both options—staying married or choosing to divorce—made me uneasy, I knew which choice gave me more hope. The thought of staying in a semi-comfortable, familiar situation suddenly became intolerable as I thought of growing old in a marriage that would just get worse over time. I was finally ready to give myself a chance at happiness. I felt strong enough to face the unknown and the challenges of divorce. I had worked to try to save the marriage, and now it was time to save me.

Lessons Learned

- People tell you exactly what you need to know. Listen to their words but more importantly, watch their actions (show me, don't tell me).
- There are basic things that make a relationship work. You won't get everything you want, but you should get what is deep down important to you and not have to compromise on the things you need in a partner.
- Don't be with someone who doesn't want to be with you.
- Neglect is a form of abuse.

When There Is No Choice

Maybe getting divorced is the last thing you wanted and expected—your partner's the one who's leaving the marriage. This scenario presents a challenge to get it together and prepare for the next step as you try to deal with your crushed ego and self-esteem.

While you had no control in the decision to divorce, you do have control over how you choose to handle the situation. It's a process, and the emotional pain is a necessary experience in order to move on and start the healing process; but be careful not to let it rule your life.

Take time to grieve the loss, and then make the choice to move on. Accepting that "it is what it is" may sound simplistic, but it can be powerful. Focus on the things you can control, and work to change your perspective from the negative to the positive. It will be as easy or difficult as you make it. Redirect your energy to the process called "divorce." It is an experience that you need to go through to create a new life and find your happiness. The best revenge comes when you eventually let go of your anger and allow happiness to blossom.

Eileen—43 years old

I was married for over twenty years, during which time we had three children who are now preteens and teenagers. Our marriage had its share of problems, but nothing I ever felt was serious enough to jeopardize our relationship. I was shocked when my husband told me he was leaving the kids and me to move in with his girlfriend. He said he was bored with our marriage and wanted to experience new adventures and people in his life. As he uttered these words, I actually dropped to my knees. I felt like he had physically punched me in the gut.

I started to recover from the shock of having my world turned upside down when I opened my eyes to the harsh reality that my soon-to-be ex was going to do everything in his power to pay our children and me as little support as possible. The lawyer's fees were outrageous, so we settled out of court for something that would give me a few months to get on my feet after working part-time as a nurse. In a six-month period, I went from a married and oblivious stay-at-home mom to a divorced single mom who had to go out and make a living to support her reconfigured family.

It's been five years now, and I have made a full financial and emotional recovery into a completely different life. Much to my surprise, despite all the financial and emotional challenges, I am happier now than I ever was in my married life. Looking back I think the hardest part for me was the complete loss of control and power I had in the situation. I was losing my husband and the trappings of our life together, and there was nothing I could do to stop it. I was angry at my ex and the complete stranger who stole him from me.

One day I woke up and the rage and self-pity I had been marinating in had finally dried up, and I felt a sense of peace. I realized I had a new life waiting for me to enjoy with my healthy children, and I was ready to stop wasting time. The surprise was that not only did I survive but I actually thrived through the experience and so did my children. I had never realized that I was unhappy in my marriage because at the time I never knew what it felt like to be truly happy. When my husband left me, it was devastating, but as time moved on, it turned out to be a blessing in disguise.

Lessons Learned

- You don't know how strong you can be until you are tested and have to rise to the occasion. Being pushed to your limits can bring out the best in who you are. Sometimes you just have to click into survival mode and do what has to be done.
- Taking charge of your life after something unexpectedly turns your world upside down can create a great sense of self-reliance and happiness.
- When something bad happens that you have no control over, your attitude and actions will determine the path of your life. You have a choice in how you will handle the inevitable bumps in the road, big and small.

Abuse

In an abusive situation you
don't have to do anything except leave.

Abusive marriages are dangerous and present a whole different set of circumstances. Physical abuse is dangerous and visible. Verbal and emotional abuse is not as visible but can be even more dangerous in the long term. On average, an abused woman leaves seven to ten times before permanently leaving a dangerous relationship. Many women who feel emotionally and financially trapped go back to their abuser because they don't have a support system to help them out of their situation. The good news is that you can get help by tapping into the resources your community offers. There are many organizations that will help abused women. They can provide safety for victims, including children, who are the most undeserving victims. Many organizations have programs that teach women how to be financially and emotionally self-sufficient so they can start a new life on their own terms.

Your local phone book should have a number for the toll-free crisis information hotline, which will give you information about places in your area that can provide shelter, food and counseling. Communities offer immediate emergency shelter and can also help you take the next step. For instance, if drugs are a problem, there are rehab programs that provide counseling to help get you clean and sober. Many programs are designed to help get you on the road toward your independence by guiding you on your career and finances and improving your self-esteem. While each state and community is different, help is out there. Picking up the phone can ultimately change your life for the better.

Counseling services may be offered at no charge or on a sliding fee schedule depending on your financial situation. Trained professionals can help you understand how the vicious cycle of abuse works, which will help you look at your situation with open eyes. Knowledge is power. It will help improve your confidence and self-esteem which will in turn enable you to protect your children and make your life work. Taking these first few steps will help you find the courage to stop compounding the damage that results from returning to your abuser.

No woman is immune from the possibility of physical or emotional abuse. Help is available to get information, resources and the determination to walk away and stand on your own two feet for good. You really can have a good life by ending a marriage that has you on terror alert 24/7; take the opportunity and make it happen. Often, the most difficult hurdle to overcome is admitting that your relationship is abusive in the first place.

Carolyn—39 years old

I was married to a man who was addicted to drugs. During our short engagement I knew he occasionally smoked marijuana at parties, but it never seemed habitual. During the early years of our marriage, we were both athletic and very involved in preparing for and running marathons together. Once we had children, a lot of our extracurricular activities came to a halt, and his substitute for feeling good and escaping was to experiment with drugs.

Life quickly started to change; he lived in his own little world of work and drugs. He didn't participate in family activities, and when he was home it was like living with Dr. Jekyll and Mr. Hyde. I would literally hold my breath when he walked through the front door, wondering which personality to brace myself for. I found myself getting very depressed as his neglect and verbal abuse intensified. After some particular nasty behavior he could always read me to know when I reached my limit and was ready to kick him out. When this happened he would routinely throw me a few crumbs of sweetness and back off the drugs for a few days. I allowed this dance to become a crazy cycle of getting pushed away and sucked right back in. I became his enabler by making his life's routine with drugs easy. I would take care of everything and leave him with little responsibility. He could count on me to care for the children, the house and the bills, and I was always around to participate in the next round of abuse.

I became sick of living in crisis mode when the terror alert was always red. A friend suggested that I join Al-Anon, and the counselors there were wonderful. The group meetings taught me that in order to beat an addiction my husband would have to get sober first and then deal with the underlying issues that got him there in the first place. By staying, I made his life too easy and gave him no reason to make that transition. After a few months of counseling, I found the strength to take the children and leave.

Breaking away was one of the hardest things to do, but unquestionably one of the best things I could ever have done. A few months after I left, he started getting help but to this day he still struggles with his addiction, but is slowly making progress. The guilt I felt for leaving him was overwhelming, but it was what I had to do for myself and my children.

A few months after my divorce, I started to understand that life didn't have to be about living in stress mode 24/7. Going through that difficult time made me appreciate life more and all the possibilities that were open to me. I had much more energy for myself, for my children and for furthering my career. In time, I gained perspective and started feeling like a whole person again, and I decided to start dating. It was a bit awkward at first, but now I'm having a great time meeting all kinds of people and I feel terrific. In my marriage, there never seemed to be any time *to have fun. The stress of erratic and abusive behavior from a husband addicted to drugs, along with the responsibilities of kids and work, had sucked the life out of me. For me, getting a divorce and learning to live my life again has been a gift not only to myself but, more importantly, to my children.*

Lessons Learned

- Verbal abuse is abuse. It's more difficult to believe or prove because there are no visible marks left on the body, but significant damage is being done.
- Any type of abuse is unacceptable. If your safety is at risk you need to leave. Your community has services to help.

Making Peace with Yourself

Most women who chose divorce and who have eventually found their happiness have no regrets:

- They feel like they did the necessary work to truly improve themselves and their relationships before giving up on their marriages. Their gut feelings told them it was all right to let go and move on.
- They had realistic views of marriage and knew that Prince Charming only lives in fairy tales.
- Their decision to divorce was not made after a blow-out or disagreement, but was a slow and gradual choice that required thought and soul-searching. Making the decision gave them a feeling of peace.
- The process temporarily turned everyone's life upside down. Their definition of everything returning to "normal" took on a whole

new meaning as they settled down into something quite different
from life as they knew it.

- The pay-off for working through the process was significant and
  worth all the hardship and growing pains.
- The recently divorced said it was necessary to spend time alone to
  get some perspective and figure out who they currently were and
  what they wanted before getting involved in another relationship.
- They experienced moments of doubt and regret for what could
  have been but realized this was normal and very important to
  grieve the loss of the person, as well as the dream, in order to move
  on. There was no escaping the pain in order to move on toward
  healing.

Attitude Is Everything

Throughout this book you will constantly be reminded that having
a healthy attitude is essential for your recovery after divorce. This is
especially true when you tackle the challenge of financially securing
your future during the process of divorce. Having a positive attitude is
even more important as you start your new life.

Through my interview process for the book, I had a unique opportunity to meet women from many walks of life. They each had different
personalities and attitudes that directly affected their emotional and
financial futures after divorce. The next few pages describe certain
stereotypes of women I came to know through my process. Think
about the type of person you want to be as you start securing and making your way into your new future.

The "Prima Donna"

She's the woman caught in a circle of dependency screaming,
"Somebody take care of me now, I deserve it!" Her divorce isn't even
final, and she's already spending her evening hours out on the town on
the prowl for a "Prince Charming" to rescue her from herself. Her

mantra is: "The first time I married for love, the next time I'm marrying for money!" During the daylight hours, she's applying all her energy and resources toward the legal battle of squeezing out more money from her ex. She's not even thinking about facing her financial responsibility. She's way too busy shopping at the mall. She spends ridiculous amounts of money on designer handbags and expensive lunches with her friends so they can complain about their lives and bad-mouth their exes.

The Prima Donna strategy pans out badly in court and in real life. Judges can't stand women with their attitudes and jewelry as they sob into their Kleenex. As far as eligible men, I can't think of any worthy bachelor who would be attracted to a woman whose main objective is a free ride. The Prima Donna may enjoy a cushy lifestyle for a few years after the divorce—until the alimony stops and the money runs out. That's when reality sets in and she realizes how much time and energy she wasted.

She could have used her resources and time wisely to get a head start on her new life with a plan to become financially independent. Instead, she squandered away her opportunity and now has to start off at a disadvantage as she scrambles to get her feet on the ground. Out of desperation, she may latch on to some shlub who is willing to take care of her. The problem is that the free ride usually has a lot of strings attached that will only create more misery and dependency.

The "Vengeful Princess Warrior"

We all know the saying: "Hell hath no fury like a woman scorned." The Vengeful Princess Warrior is the woman who proves that women can be more vicious and conniving than men. She cleans out all financial accounts and makes a mad dash for the hills. If she needs to stick around, she is premeditative and finds inventive strategies for pocketing thousands of dollars without her husband's knowledge before the divorce is final.

What she doesn't know is that her scheming is quite obvious and will potentially hurt any chance of her getting what she deserves. For example, a woman who has a game plan to fulfill her domestic and cosmetic dreams just before asking her husband for a divorce is in for a surprise. She's the one who redecorates her whole house, gets her teeth capped and breasts augmented, and for her pain and misery buys herself expensive pieces of jewelry. When this type of case goes to court, a judge will be very displeased with her recent acquisitions and enhancements. Once the marital estate is divided, there is a good chance she will have to pay for her new expenses herself because her timing was suspect. Even worse, she might be asking for some type of alimony in front of a judge who is already disgusted with her behavior.

The other type of princess warrior is out for spite because her husband has left her for another woman. She has tried to ease her pain through wholesale and retail therapy with a vengeance as she happily creates a huge credit card debt. When it comes time for the divorce, there will be little understanding or empathy for her reckless swiping of plastic. A judge will likely make her responsible for her shopping spree debt, which may take her years to pay off.

Unfortunately, the Vengeful Princess Warrior has not learned that reckless behavior will not only hurt her financially but also emotionally. Her anger is getting the best of her, and she will suffer the consequences. The princess needs to have an intervention for her reckless behavior because it will likely risk her financial and emotional future. Regardless of the situation, she needs to get a grip on her anger and try to take the high road. Being honest and fair with her spouse with what she realistically and legally deserves will positively serve her future. Smarter actions and a better attitude will help her achieve a better outcome. She will also like herself better for handling a difficult situation with grace and dignity. This holds true especially when she has continued contact with him after the divorce as they raise their children together.

Lessons Learned

- There is a great saying: "Your morals and principles are only as good as when they are put to the test." Try to remember this when you're about to do something out of anger; it will help get you back on the right path.
- Bad behavior will bring you bad results.
- A judge will easily see through any type of premeditative actions that affect the marital estate.
- Get a reality check, nobody owes you anything. Don't count on a judge to reward you a settlement that will set you up for life. If you are lucky enough to get some form of alimony, use your time and money wisely.
- The sooner you take financial responsibility for your life, the sooner you can start taking actions to make it work on your terms.

The "Guilty Conscience"

The woman with the guilty conscience lets her judgment cloud the divorce negotiations. She's the woman who lets her husband take full advantage of her financially because she is guilt-ridden for ending the marriage. Unfortunately, once reality sets in, she realizes what she forfeited after it's too late to fight for a more equitable settlement. What she failed to realize is that sometimes the action that ended a marriage is simply the straw that broke the camel's back after years of problems and misery.

Lessons Learned

- Don't let your guilt get the best of you and allow yourself to be taken advantage of during your divorce.

- Remember that your husband most likely played a significant role in the destruction of your marriage. Stand up and fight for what you deserve.

"Glenda the Good"

She's the woman whose conscience helps guide her actions to do what is fair. She tries not to take too much advantage of a situation and remembers that the cost of a legal battle might cancel out any possible financial or emotional victory. She listens to her lawyer carefully but makes the final decisions herself. She understands that her lawyer has an interest in prolonging the battle because it lines his pockets.

This woman is able to let her conscience evaluate the big picture and balance the financial and emotional factors. She chooses the path of less chaos and destruction while standing her ground firmly for what she realistically deserves and is legally entitled to. This is especially important when children are involved. Her conscience guides her to fight for what her children need without dragging them into a bloody legal battle that can last for years. She understands how detrimental a vicious battle can be, causing stress and anxiety that will directly affect her children.

Glenda the Good makes a choice to call off her bloodhound attorneys. While she knows she could have milked her husband for all he was worth, she knows she couldn't live with herself after the bloodbath. Her conscience tells her she has no claim to someone else's fortune even though she could have tapped into it legally. She settles out of court for something that is fair which gives her a good head start in her new life. Glenda the Good walks away from divorce with her pride and dignity intact. Her choices and actions attract many wonderful things and people into her new life.

Lessons Learned

- A smart woman will do her best to set aside her emotions when making decisions regarding the business of divorce. Thinking smart will minimize the emotional and financial toll.
- Fight for what you deserve as you take the high road; your actions during the divorce will spill over into your new life.

The "Victim"

She is the woman your heart breaks for, whose life is filled with heartache and broken promises. She's dealt with infidelity, drug addictions, gambling addictions and abuse. She has little emotional or financial support and is faced with the daunting task of supporting herself, and maybe even children, solo. She feels like she's swimming in a tank filled with sharks and can barley keep her head above water.

She can easily fall into victim mode when she's left with huge debt, no money in the bank, and no chance for alimony or child support after her husband has disappeared. Whether or not she's a self-imposed or legitimate victim, life moves on and she needs to find a way to survive financially.

Lessons Learned

- Initially, the majority of women suffer more financially from the breakup of a marriage than men. It may take years to recover a certain lifestyle, but women do better overall post divorce after adjusting to their new set of circumstances.
- When forced to reach their potential women accomplish far more than they ever thought possible.

- Recovery starts the moment action is taken to adjust to a new situation. Many women say that once they opened their hearts and minds, it wasn't hard to make the choice to go from "victim" mentality to "survivor" mentality.

The "Survivor"

She's the woman who goes through the divorce experience feeling like a contestant on a reality TV show. She describes being thrown into a situation where she had to hit the ground running with limited resources. While protecting her young, she had to search for shelter, food and a way to survive during the worst possible storm she ever experienced.

She felt like a caged animal that had finally been set free into the unknown wild with limited skills. Every night she would watch over her children as they slept, filled with anxiety about how she was going to get through the next day. Her feelings continued week after week as she worked like a dog and barely got by. The weight of the responsibility was almost too much when she realized her family's survival was all up to her, but there was no time to think about it.

Instead of cursing her new circumstances, she knew the only thing to do was figure out how to make it work. After some time, she started to get a handle on things and carved out a place for her family in this wild new world. Her success started giving her a sense of control over her life. It was a hard test, but she felt she had passed with much hard work and a positive attitude toward success.

The survivor is a woman who goes from being a scared little housewife to a successful provider and strong mother for her children. She starts to enjoy and live her life instead of just surviving it. Her prize is her independence and happiness she never experienced in her old life until she was forced to embark on a journey of financial and emotional survival.

Lessons Learned

- Women who have good outcomes with their divorces and "afterlife" have positive attitudes toward life and money. They see their future the way they want it to be regardless of their situation and make a choice to figure out a way to make it on their own.

Keep Your Eye on the Ball

So it's time to bite the bullet and move into the process of uncoupling. You feel like your head is about to explode as you sift through the paperwork in your divorce packet and come face-to-face with something called the financial affidavit. It's a piece of paper asking you to fill out every financial detail of your life. It's the absolute last thing you think you're capable of doing because you're barely functioning in your emotionally overloaded state. At any moment, you don't know if you're going to cry or throw something across the room, and now you're being asked to sit down and crunch numbers? Yeah, right.

Unfortunately, you don't have a choice; there is no getting around this business of uncoupling. Taking a mental leave of absence during this critical part of divorce will jeopardize your future. There will be plenty of time to work on your emotional state but right now you have to compartmentalize what's in your head so you can hunker down and zero in on your finances. If you can't do it alone, get some help from your attorney or a family member to get focused on the tasks ahead of you.

The key to succeeding in the business of divorce is to keep your cool and remain objective. Move forward steadily, but with vigilance and eyes wide open. Taking stock of your finances and how these might change is an important next step that you need to take seriously. The next chapter will help prepare you to work out your financial situation. Getting familiar with your finances will give you the tools and confidence to effectively manage your divorce and make adjustments for the future.

Financial Fitness and Survival

*Right now I have enough money
to last me the rest of my life—unless I buy something.*

—Jackie Mason

Contrary to what many people believe, men do much better financially than women after divorce. Women rarely walk off with lifetime alimony or a big pile of cash in their bank accounts; they're lucky if they can afford to stay in the marital home. All this came as quite a shock to me. I thought my situation would leave my kids and me financially protected well into the future, but I was wrong.

My ex and I are chiropractors and opened an office soon after we married. We started from nothing and after a few lean, hard years we created a very successful practice. In time, we hired associates to cover our office hours, and the practice ran like a well-oiled machine and I was able to spend more time with our baby. When we had our second child, I took a back seat at the practice to stay home with the kids. My husband was working part time to manage the business end of the practice and would occasionally see patients.

When it came to our divorce, I lost my share in our practice. The judge felt my ex would be more successful with the business because he still had a physical presence there. I had to sign over full ownership to him in return for a pittance.

Now my ex would enjoy significant income for years to come with minimal effort, whereas three years later our youngest was entering kindergarten and my alimony was cut off. I was suddenly at a huge financial disadvantage. I realized that going to work for someone else would yield a fraction of the income I was accustomed to while having to work twice the hours. Starting a new practice was out of the question as that would require spending too much time away from my children. I had to be creative and find a way to make money and make time for my kids. I now have two careers, one as a chiropractor for vacation relief work and the other in real estate. They both give me flexibility to raise my kids but it's a struggle. I work harder than I ever have before and still make substantially less. The good news is that I'm happier than I've ever been before.

Lessons Learned

- Don't assume you are going to get what you want or need financially. Chances are it won't happen, so you better have an alternate plan to make your life work.

Divorce is a great teacher, and the experience can build character as it tests you to your core. The lessons can be painful but the end results can change your life for the better—depending on your perspective and attitude. A tough lesson to learn is that life is hard and not always fair. A meditation teacher of mine talked about this very idea. She said once you accept the fact that life is unfair, everything in your world suddenly becomes sweeter. You start to appreciate things more and look at problems as opportunities to grow and learn.

That's exactly how I started to view my divorce. It wasn't fair that my life took this course, but it did. I knew that financial struggles were in my future, and I had to get my act together. The hardest part was dealing with my new reality at a time when my emotional sanity was teetering on the edge. Rather than freaking out about it, I tried to use my energy and resources to figure out ways to make my new life work.

Life is a series of problems. Do we want
to moan about them or solve them?

—M. Scott Peck

Financial Boot Camp

Your first step as you move into the divorce process is to take stock of your financial situation and work out your financial survival strategy. There's a good chance you're going to have to get back into the work force or find a better job that pays more money. As if this isn't enough, you may not be able to afford to live in your home, and eventually, you may have to move into something more affordable. Things will be turned upside down and you'll find that you might need to take a few steps backward before moving forward again. While taking on this challenge, evaluate your attitude toward money and financial responsibility.

As you prepare to untie the many entanglements of your marriage, you need to get organized and have a sense of fairness as you move into the process. Have a realistic idea of what you are entitled to according to the laws in your state. This will help you get through the process more efficiently and prevent a lawyer from emotionally taking advantage of you just to milk your marital estate. Pick and choose your battles wisely to maximize your chances for a positive outcome.

This thing called divorce can be a marathon so prepare to have some stamina. I know too many women who later regretted settling on terms that were unfair simply because they wanted to get it over with. Going into Victim, Guilt, Prima Donna or Warrior mode is not going to help when you enter into negotiations with your husband. Put aside who did what to whom. Your economic well-being depends on your attitude and your ability to separate your emotions from the facts.

Educate yourself in preparation for the actual legal divorce and for your new life flying solo. Your lawyer can't save you by himself. You'll need to be an active participant who provides answers and information on request if you want to keep your costs down and get what is rightfully yours.

If you have no idea where your money is, how it is invested, managed or spent, it's time to get a clue. I know some women who never open the mail unless it's an invitation to a party! It's time to start paying attention if you've been out of your financial loop. Start doing undercover detective work by opening the mail and watching the money that comes in and out of your household. Go through the file cabinets where your husband keeps the financial records, make copies and take notes.

You can get overwhelmed with this process because you have to focus on business when you are running on emotional overload. The good news is that by doing your research and understanding your finances, you'll start to feel more in control of your financial future. You'll also start to feel empowered by your newly acquired knowledge.

I'm embarrassed to admit I was clueless about our household finances. I had never been good at numbers and had been happy to give all the responsibilities to my husband. I was lazy and never very interested in learning the details. When I realized my marriage was in trouble, I started to pay attention, starting with balancing our checking account. I gave myself a crash course on what we had and what we owed. I even met with our financial advisor and read some books to get a better understanding of investments. When financial statements came in the mail, I started to scrutinize them until they made sense.

A friend who was recently divorced gave me the name of her attorney and some good advice. She told me that as soon as I could I should make copies or take out of the house all financial records for the last few years. I chose to make copies rather than make our financial records disappear. It was a big job but I did it over a few days after getting a list of what I needed. I was grateful to have done this work while things were calm.

A few weeks later, my husband hired an attorney who advised him to clean out all of our important financial files and everything was gone. While it was still a shock, I kept my cool because I had a lot of what I needed. I was prepared by the time I had my first meeting with my lawyer, which saved a lot of time and money and allowed us to move forward quickly. Here are the things you need to do that will help you transition into uncoupling.

The Bank Accounts:
- If you don't have a separate account in your name, get one immediately! Go to a different bank or branch for extra security.
- It's standard practice to withdraw half of what is in your joint savings account and put that portion in your new account. Try not to spend it until you have an official division of assets, but at least you are safeguarding your interest.
- If things are amicable, leave enough money in a joint checking account to cover shared bills like rent and utilities.
- If your paycheck is directly deposited into your joint account, reroute this to your new separate account immediately.

The Credit Cards:
- If you don't have a separate credit card in your name only, get one immediately!
- Once you have established credit in your own name, it's a good idea to cancel the credit cards that are held jointly. Make sure you tell your husband you are doing this.
- If you feel that things will remain amicable, you can both set limits on what you can charge each month. Be careful, though, because you have no control over this. If he gets vengeful and goes on a spending revenge, it's not just his debt but yours too. It's safer

for both of you to get your own separate cards and cancel what you have jointly. This will ensure that your credit does not get ruined and you remain in good standing for your future.

Insurance Policies and Payments:
- Get declaration pages on all of your policies with account numbers, premiums, payment dates and what your coverage is.
- Contact each company and let them know you are getting a divorce and that no policy should be cancelled without your consent. Most companies would like a notarized letter with such notification.
- Pay particular attention to your health, car and life insurance. Your spouse can easily cancel them or purposely not pay the premiums with the goal of getting you dropped from the company, leaving you with no coverage.
- To avoid any problems, be responsible for paying your own premiums.

Debt:
- Your total credit card debt.
- Mortgage and equity lines.
- Student loans.
- Car loans.
- Make sure income taxes and property taxes have been paid. I know one woman who was awarded her house during the divorce. When she had to sell it, she found out her husband hadn't paid the taxes in over three years. She was over $20,000 in debt. By the time she realized this, it was too late to do anything about it.

Your Divorce Folder:
Below is a summary of what you should provide a lawyer with the first time you meet:

- A recent pay stub of your husband's paycheck.
- Copies of both your tax returns for the past few years.
- A list of all your investments, including stocks, bonds, deeds to

property, both of your 401Ks and mutual funds.
- Copies of recent bank statements.
- Insurance policies.
- Mortgage and papers from recent home transactions (refinancing or appraisal).
- Car loans.
- Wills or trusts.
- Current real estate taxes.
- Monthly budget.
- Current debt balances. (If you have already separated, get the balance as of date of separation.)

The more information you can dig up and prepare in an orderly fashion the better. If you have a significant marital estate, you will need more information.

When working with attorneys, there is a term called "discovery"—the process used by lawyers to get information from the other side or from a third party. Try to save time and money by getting additional information on your own, or asking your husband to cooperate by providing the necessary information. Sharing information will save you both legal fees and allow both of you to keep more of your marital estate. You may need to obtain some things with the professional help of your attorney, but hopefully there will be full cooperation from the other side.

Squirrelly Stashes

When you feel like your back is up against the wall, you might be surprised by some of the things you and your spouse are capable of doing. I'm talking about hoarding money, jewelry and precious art. It's like watching squirrels gathering acorns for the winter. My interviews have shown that men and women are equally guilty in their participation in these types of activities. One guy went so far as to cut a hole in the drywall in his closet to stash a few thousand dollars. He patched and painted to cover the mess until he was ready to move out of his house with his treasure in hand.

I'm not advocating this type of behavior. It can come back to haunt you and may cause more harm than good. However, some steps will be necessary to help prevent valuable property and money from disappearing permanently from your marital estate by your soon-to-be ex. Regardless of how amicable or nasty you expect your divorce to get, it's time to be a little suspicious of his actions so make sure you do some homework.

Hopefully you'll have a good idea of what the inventory is and where it can be found. Start making records of items worth more than $500 that are in safety deposit boxes, coat pockets, shoes, home safes and any imaginative place you know of. Don't forget any money that is marital that you think might be in secret accounts in Switzerland or somehow handled by his friends or family. Do some undercover work and dig up as much information as possible. If you at least know of these assets, your lawyer will have the legal means to get further information.

While you are still married, your spouse can spend or take and sell any of these items at any time and it's all legal. However, once you have an official separation date, if either party takes things of value, they can be held liable for their actions—but evidence is needed.

It's your job to take pictures of these items as well as compile a list of all valuables and amounts of money. With large amounts of cash, spread the bills out with visible dollar amounts and the day's newspaper in the background with a clear shot of the paper's date. With other valuables that might be in a safety deposit box, write a list of items and what you think they are worth. Have a friend or bank officer compare what they see to your list. Ask them to sign and date the accuracy of your list after their review. Having someone witness the existence of such items with a documented date can be helpful if testimony is needed in court at a later date.

This all might feel very sneaky and underhanded, but it's not. It's about protecting your best interests. Think of it as a preventive measure that you hopefully won't need to utilize. If you don't do this and your spouse wipes out all of the stashes, you will have little chance to recover any of it.

Always remember the saying "All is fair in love and war." Hopefully it won't be an all-out war but remember that it's still a divorce. It's a very stressful time and someone you know, including yourself, can act totally out of character. Do all you can to avoid getting the short end of the stick. There's nothing wrong with preparing for your worst case scenario and fighting for what is fair. If you start feeling pangs of guilt about your preparation and preventative measures, remember your spouse is probably out there doing the same things as he looks out for his best interests, not yours.

WARNING

Always remember the double-edged sword! You are taking these preventive measures to make sure you're not placed at a disadvantage, which is fine, but remember that anything you do that looks or smells suspicious can and will be used against you!

Men and Money

When dealing with and preparing for the financial aspects of divorce, men do very well. Their caveman biological programming kicks in to high gear and they focus in on one thing: the kill. I'm certainly not saying that women can't be killer warriors in this situation, but there is a difference in coping styles. Often, women can get bogged down with the emotions of the divorce, causing a delay in their ability to get focused on the "business" of divorce. Many men, however, often click into survival mode immediately as they leave all emotion behind and zero into "what's ours is mine" mode.

Some men slip into a temporary state of convenient amnesia as they forget you were once the woman they loved and shared a life with. His competitive nature can cause him to forget that you are the mother of his children. You've become his opponent, and he needs to beat you at all costs. This is especially true if they are the ones who have been left. When it comes to money, prepare yourself to meet a side of your spouse you've never seen before. You might be surprised to find that *"Hell hath no fury like a man scorned."*

If you're lucky enough to be on amicable terms with your spouse, you still need to pay particular attention to what's in your best interests. When it comes to the financial aspects of divorce, always remember that you are playing on opposite teams. Don't go into negotiations trusting that your ex will do what's best for you. It's okay to go in with good intentions as long as you've done your own homework. You must know what's fair and equitable in your own mind without your spouse trying to convince you of his opinion.

This is where many women get into trouble. Listen to what your spouse has to say with your ears open and your mouth shut. Never agree to anything on the spot. Tell him you will consider his points but first you need time to consider what he's presented. Make sure you have good people around you, whether it's hired professionals or family members, to discuss the situation with.

You may feel comfortable telling your spouse the actions you are about to take as you move through the business of uncoupling. If you're in a hostile or uncomfortable situation, you'll need to prepare for the divorce discreetly, but you should notify him about any major changes you make that will directly affect him, for instance, canceling joint credit cards. While this might feel uncomfortable, it's all perfectly legal and all about protecting your assets and future. It's not uncommon for divorces that start off amicably to turn ugly very quickly once you start talking about dividing property and money.

Many women will probably need to do their preparatory work without their spouse knowing. Be careful to keep your lists and inventory in a safe place or with a best friend or family member. The last thing you want to do is inflame a stressful situation that can make your spouse even thirstier for revenge and "the kill."

Peaceful Resolution

Many people are able to work out the financial business of divorce without spending their marital estate on legal fees. A peaceful resolution to divorce starts with a cooperative effort to compile all financial records and information. After reviewing all assets and liabilities, the couple either agrees to fairly divide their marital estate to the satisfaction of both parties or they use a mediator to find a fair resolution. Not only can you save a huge amount of money in legal fees but you will both preserve your emotional sanity. This is even more important when children are involved. This cooperation is possible when

- There is very little money or property to squabble about;
- There are no child custody issues;
- Couples have enough respect for each other and trust one another to work out what each feels to be a fair division of marital assets. The latter is a unique situation but it can—and does—happen, especially when the divorce isn't a direct result of abuse, lies or infidelity.

Taking Stock

Now that you are moving toward divorce, you start to realize you can no longer count on your husband's income or his management of money as you learn to fly solo. This can significantly cut into your lifestyle and produce a lot of anxiety about your future. Knowledge regarding your household finances and the flow of your money will be the first step toward taking charge of your life. Believe it or not, most people have no idea how much it really costs to run their household and whether or not there is money left over at the end of the month. My lawyer gave me an assignment to write down all of our household expenses. I was shocked and embarrassed to realize just how clueless I was.

At first the task seemed daunting, but after putting some time in, I realized it wasn't difficult to get a handle on our money matters. It was a matter of some basic accounting, budgeting and developing some organizational skills to get the bills paid. Once I pulled it all together and saw what I was dealing with, I felt calmer and more in control.

The best way to start is to get a clean sheet of paper, a pencil and a calculator. Write down all family expenses and all of the money that comes into the household. Now figure out what you will need to cover your expenses without your husband's income—and while you do this remember to keep breathing. By having things down on paper, you'll be able to see where you have some wiggle room and where you can tighten your belt. Some of you will need to go back to work or find a way to bring in more income, depending on your financial and legal situation. For those of you who need to educate yourselves on personal money matters, the next few pages will be a good guide to get you started.

Monthly Expenses

Household
The Necessities
- MORTGAGE OR RENT—If you're the one who has to move out, changing residence can be one of the most difficult transitions. Evaluate your situation carefully and see what you can afford. Getting a roommate or temporarily moving in with family or friends may be your best option in the short term.
- UTILITIES—telephone (home and cell), water, electric, cable, Internet.
- GROCERIES.
- INSURANCE—Homeowners, flood, renter's protection, umbrella, etc.
- TAXES.
- OTHER—condo or association fees, cleaning service, alarm system, maintenance contracts like pest control, lawn or pool.

Transportation:
- *Car payments
- *Insurance

- *Gas
- *Maintenance
- *Garage
- Public Transportation
- Tolls
- Taxis

*It may be time to re-evaluate your situation by getting a less expensive car, finding a car pool or opting for public transportation.

Entertainment:
- Shows, movies, concerts
- Books, magazines
- Vacation

It's important to get out there and be social but be reasonable and learn how to make it work without running up too much debt. Once in a while it will become necessary for your sanity to go out and splurge even if it's just for short-term gratification.

Personal Maintenance:
- Clothing
- Health and dental insurance, eyewear, prescriptions, therapy, doctor's visits
- Hair: cut, color and style
- Makeup
- Spa: massage, manicure, pedicure, waxing, facial, etc.
- Gym: very important for health and self-esteem so find a cheaper gym before you give up a membership.

Feeling good about yourself is very important to your recovery right now. Cut back on things you can do yourself like your nails but try to keep that hair appointment.

Miscellaneous:
• Savings
• Loans

Money-Saving Suggestions

Consider things you can cut back on, at least for a while, as you get your life back together:

• Can you do without the cell phone or cable TV? If you don't watch the premium movie channels or use DSL, cancel them, or shop for a cheaper service.
• There are ways you can save on your electricity. Call your local power company for different options and suggestions.
• Shop around for phone carriers that offer the best deal. If you have two or more phone lines, try to get by on just one.
• Take advantage of grocery coupons in the paper and on the Internet. Watch for free product samples.
• Shop around for the best rates on insurance. You can also lower your premiums by raising your deductibles.
• Buy clothing and linens only when there are sales. You can save up to 75 percent on clothing when you buy as stores are clearing out merchandise for the next season.
• Bring your lunch to work rather than going out.
• Carpool to save on fuel, mileage, and wear and tear of your vehicle.
• Do you have a cleaning service? Start cleaning the house yourself or space the cleaning service out an extra week.
• Consider getting a roommate.
• Remember, the little things add up. Starbucks coffee at four bucks a shot is really not a daily necessity in life! You could easily save $120 dollars a month. Get your caffeine fix at home.

> Make sure you put aside money in savings plans such as a money market account for quarterly and yearly payments on insurance, taxes, maintenance contracts, etc.

Start saving money in that separate bank account you opened for some of the one-time expenditures you'll encounter as you transition into your new life:

One-time expenses:
- Lawyer
- Mediator
- Accountant
- Moving expenses and storage
- New furniture

These expenses will be a guess at best, but it will give you a good ballpark figure of what to expect so you'll have a better idea how to plan.

Budgeting in Some TLC

Living through this time can be emotionally and physically draining, but you are not alone. There are many women in your shoes, feeling the same financial crunch and anxiety. Joining forces with other single parents or recently divorced people creates a network of people you can count on even if it's just to have a good chat over coffee. Reach out to your community through religious organizations and groups for single parents or divorced people to make new friends where you can help and support each other.

Sometimes pampering yourself may be necessary to lift your spirits and maintain a positive attitude as you move through your divorce.

With a little planning, you may be able to create a slush fund to give yourself some desperately needed TLC. Bagging your lunch and having a can of tuna for dinner can help you pay for a massage, weekend get-away or extra session with your therapist when you really need it.

If this is not possible, rent a movie or take a walk in the park to decompress and escape for a while. Take the opportunity to be good to yourself during your transition by finding creative ways to save up and have fun without reckless swiping of your credit card.

Lifestyle Sticker Shock

Now that you have a better idea of what you need to cover your monthly nut, how does it look? There's a good chance you're in shock as you realize just how much it takes to keep your world turning. The harsh reality is that women's standard of living can go down as much as 40 percent after a divorce due to the loss of their spouse's income. Making matters more challenging are lawyer fees, bad debt, credit problems and child care issues.

You will probably experience a change in your lifestyle temporarily, and it's okay. Many women recover after a few years with some smart planning and budgeting. You may need to move to a less expensive neighborhood, find a roommate, change careers, find a job or go back to school to increase your earning potential. Now is not the time to feel embarrassed about asking for help from friends and family. Don't hesitate to ask for a loan with no or low interest from someone close to you who can afford it. If that's not possible, credit cards might be your only option to help you transition into your new life. Using your card wisely for basic needs and investing in your future (such as furthering your education) is a necessary debt that will help you get by and help you create a better future.

Taking Financial Responsibility

It's time to get in the driver's seat of your financial future because it's all up to you now. If you find yourself in serious debt, Consumer Credit Counseling Services (CCCS) is an excellent nonprofit organization that can help you resolve any immediate crisis and then help you set up a strategy to create a healthy financial future. The organization's main goal is to help you learn to help yourself become financially independent.

Depending on your resources, you might find the advice of financial advisers or certified financial planners very helpful. They can assess your new financial profile and help you develop a budget to live within your means. They can also develop a strategy of investing to help ensure your financial future. Whatever your resources, find the counseling to help you get back on your feet. Always remember that you are totally capable of handling your finances by yourself—don't ever give away that power.

A vocational counselor can give you career advice to help you find a job or make a higher income. These professionals help you look at all your options and create some goals, then show you how you can reach those goals. Staying at a dead-end job or working two jobs to make ends meet will only make you feel like you are getting nowhere fast. Divorce forces many women to step out into the job market without a financial safety net. Many said it was difficult, but their situation forced them to achieve success levels in their jobs that they never thought were possible. Initially, many experienced financial hardship by going back to school or starting over with a new career, but the long-term rewards were well worth it.

All of this can be quite challenging but workable with the right attitude and planning. Try your best to channel your anger and nervous energy into productive ways to start creating your economic stability. It's time to be proactive and visualize where you want to be. If you see it, you will likely get to where you want to be.

Candice—32 years old

When I was twenty-nine years old, my husband left me for a stripper. Suddenly, I was alone with my two young boys and thousands of dollars in credit card debt from charges at the Pink Pussycat. I had no close family to ask for help or any kind of support. Life was looking grim. I realized my receptionist job was not going to be enough to even pay the rent. Looking into my two sons' eyes when I put them to bed at night gave me the motivation to find a way to get us out of our mess. I needed help.

The first thing I did was ask for an advance on my paycheck. I had been working for a gynecologist for the past two years, he knew I was a good employee and was happy to help me out. The extra money was just a bandage on a gaping wound, and I needed a long-term plan to pay for my household expenses and day care. For a quick fix, I sold all my jewelry, including my engagement and wedding rings for cash that would get us by for a few months, but it still wasn't enough. I realized that my only option in order to continue living in the same neighborhood and keep my children in the same school was to get a roommate. I had a girlfriend who was struggling financially, so I proposed a deal. She would pay me what she could afford for rent and fill in for the rest by helping me with my children. She was a waitress with flexible hours so it worked out for all of us.

My next step was to figure out how I was going to handle my monstrous credit card debt. A friend of mine recommended a company that deals with debt consolidation. I was able to get all of my debt down to one bill and one low payment where I wasn't getting killed by the interest rate. My financial nightmare was starting to look more manageable.

Now that the immediate fires were put out, I had to figure out what I was going to do with the rest of my life. Being a receptionist was not going to cut it; I needed more money and mental stimulation. I was always interested in the work done in my doctor's office. There was a woman who came into the office three days a week to conduct diagnostic testing with ultrasound. I asked her out to lunch to find out how she became qualified to do her job and if she liked the work. By the end of our lunch, I had the name of a school and information on how to get financial aid to pay for tuition.

The next few years were crazy. I felt like I was performing a juggling act between working all day to pay the bills, going to school at night, studying and taking care of my kids. I was in a constant state of tired. It was also hard on my kids, but we all survived. We cut back significantly on spending money for entertainment and found our fun in simple things. I didn't have a lot of time to give them, but when I did it was quality time. We set up treasure hunts, took nature walks and stayed home playing board games. We cooked together and found many creative ways to make tuna fish and ground beef tasty and exciting.

I earned my degree. The doctor I had worked with for years gave me a great recommendation, as did the woman who helped me get started. I began working for two different doctors' offices, making my own hours. I love the work and I make good money, which gives me great peace in my life knowing that I'm in control and doing a great job. I have much more time to spend with my kids and we are all doing well.

That crazy time in my life was very difficult, but my kids and I really pulled together. We created a bond that can never be broken. I'm still amazed at how much fun we had together when we were just barely getting by. We have a greater appreciation for our lifestyle now, but more importantly, for each other.

"Space Cadet" Warning

During your divorce, there will be moments of brain overload resulting from the amount of energy required of you. On top of your daily responsibilities at home and work, in your spare time you are required to present and contemplate your financial situation. All of this work and planning will directly impact your financial outcome as you end your married life and move forward. You'll also need to squeeze in some time to consult with your lawyer, accountant and other professionals as you try to wrap up the process of divorce.

The stress from your undercover work and anticipation of your life being "shaken and stirred" can easily produce a mental meltdown. Don't be surprised if your "I forgot" list includes: important appointments, picking up your children, where you put your keys or parked the car, and that something you left on the stove that caught fire. You just won't be operating on all cylinders. This can be annoying and sometimes dangerous.

Stress has a chemical effect on your brain that can affect your thinking and judgment. Prepare yourself to experience space cadet moments, and remember to forgive yourself when they happen. Your normal faculties will return once you get a handle on your situation. Try using extra preventative measures like rechecking your calendar and reviewing your day and actions to help minimize "space cadet mode."

Once you have your finances in order—or at least have an idea on how you'll be affected financially—you'll be in a stronger position as you move into the legal aspects of your divorce. However, the actual legal process will still be challenging. You are entering a world of words and procedures you may have never heard before. The next chapter will give you a good idea of the process and how it works—both for and against you.

Chapter

3

The Three-Ring Legal Circus

A woman is like a tea bag. You never know
how strong she is until she gets in hot water.

—Eleanor Roosevelt

Okay, you are at the point where divorce is imminent, and it's time to get on with the actual legal process. You are feeling vulnerable and more anxious than ever before as your heart races and you move into a process you know very little about. There is no sugarcoating it, the stakes are high, from child custody to money issues. The legal process can draw on your deepest reserves financially, physically and emotionally.

Many women are quick to admit that keeping their cool during the legal battles wasn't always easy. However, when they kept their emotional issues out of the mix, they were able to think more clearly and stay focused on the important issues of their case, which made them more effective and successful.

This chapter will teach you how to find the right lawyer and take the mystery out of the legal process with a step-by-step guide from serving papers to a possible trial. This new knowledge will minimize your fear, stress and regret factors, while building up your strength and confidence as you move through this part of your divorce journey. The goal is to keep your sense of humor, sanity and protect your best interests as you navigate your way through a sea of uncertainty and absurdity called the "Divorce Zone."

Points to remember when working with your spouse through your legal divorce:

- If a man ended the marriage because he fell out of love or found another woman, you might have an advantage when dealing with the business of divorce. Some of the men admitted to feelings of guilt, which made them more generous and cooperative than usual. Some women have capitalized on this guilt and have done very well for themselves by biting their tongue and moving forward with the process. Remember what Ivana Trump said, "Don't get mad dahling, get everything."
- If you chose to leave your husband or were unfaithful, prepare for the worst and hope for the best. Hell hath no fury like a man's annihilated ego. Not knowing where to go with his emotions, many men will do what they are programmed to do when put into a corner—fight till the very end.
- If your husband is a jock, and loves sports and the glory of victory, you could be in for a ride. He will take his thirst for winning into the halls of justice, where you are no longer the woman he used to love or the mother of his children. You are simply one thing: the enemy. Nothing will stop him from his victory, whatever he thinks that might be. The expression about winning the battle or the war is something to keep in mind. The little skirmishes between the two of you are useless and could be harmful. One guy admitted setting his wife up to say something that would be used against her in court. Keep your mouth shut and let your lawyer do the work if you are in this type of situation.
- Regardless of the breakup scenario, some men I spoke with felt like they were being reasonable with a settlement offer, only to be rejected. What resulted was an ugly court battle that seemed to nullify the outcome for both because of lawyers' fees. Educate

yourself about the law and your rights by finding a good lawyer who will work with you and give you honest answers. Fight for what you deserve and need, not what you want. Seriously consider settlement offers before turning them down. On the other hand, don't give in just because you want it to be over. Don't let your spouse convince you he is being fair; convince yourself by getting the facts from a professional. Some men I talked to admitted that they tried to take advantage of their wives by offering things that sounded good. All the while they had their fingers crossed, hoping to settle because they knew they would have to give up significantly more if it went to court.

Divorce in the Real World

The Dueling Spouses + The Lawyers
+ The Judge = Costly Chaos in a Three-Ring Circus

The family court system is far from perfect, and it's nothing like what you see on TV or in the movies. While there are rules, procedure and laws, there is also "the human factor." The ideal model of divorce court is for a judge to have absolutely no bias. However, in the real world they are still regular people carrying their own baggage into the courtroom, which colors how they see the world. In the end, a trial is nothing more than one human judging another human. Most people who walk out of a trial are not satisfied with the ruling. When they go home and think of the financial and emotional cost, it hardly seemed worth the trouble.

I am still paying off lawyer's bills from a divorce that went on a path of reckless abandon. One of my biggest mistakes was using my attorney as an emotional crutch. Seeing a licensed therapist to handle my emotional issues would have been a lot cheaper and smarter. I wish I had been more prepared to manage my lawyer as I jumped into the legal world's three-ring circus.

Looking back I blame myself and my ex for engaging in an acrimonious battle that was fueled by both of our attorneys. The end result was a diminished marital estate after they milked our bank accounts in the name of litigation. To make matters worse, we had a judge who was lazy and on the verge of retirement. He left us with a final judgment that was incomplete and open for individual interpretation. The end result was years of more litigation in a system that easily transferred our assets into our lawyers' cushy bank accounts.

From negotiations to a tedious legal procedure and a trial, I have become too familiar with concepts such as mediation, deposition, financial affidavits, interrogatories, temporary relief, and on and on. With time, perspective and a drained bank account, it has become clear to me that there is a way to do divorce and a way not to. Luckily, most divorce cases settle out of court without a judge.

There are arguments for and against taking a divorce to trial. Some lawyers believe that having a judge who is knowledgeable and objective is the best way to preserve your rights. They feel that too many people compromise on what they legally deserve because they don't know the law and settle for the sake of getting it over with. When the dust settles, many women say they regret giving in when the reality of their new world hits them, especially when there are child custody issues and complex assets and debts. The other side of the coin is that many lawyers love going to court with their clients because it means more money in their pockets. The process can be nothing more than a gamble because you are letting a complete stranger decide what is best for you and your children.

Listen to your attorney's opinion but then take a few steps back to evaluate your unique situation. First, can you afford everything involved to prepare for a trial, and do your issues justify the expense? Sometimes a trial will be necessary, but outside of some special circumstances, most professionals (including honest attorneys) will tell you to do your best to settle out of court and save yourself from significant emotional and financial hardship. The key is to have knowledgeable people around you to help you and your spouse reach a settlement. A compromise is when both parties walk away from the table feeling like they gave something up to keep something important.

Hopefully, you've already done all your financial homework as described in chapter 2 and you've created a divorce folder filled with information you'll need as you move forward.

Finding Good Legal Advice

The divorce zone can involve many different factors: children, stepchildren, significant assets, debt and inheritance. The list can go on and on or it can be as simple as who gets the couch and the goldfish. The cost of a divorce attorney can be significant but necessary. However, finding and working with the right one in the long run can be essential to maintaining your financial and emotional health. Everyone will have their unique situation that will determine their legal needs.

The "On Call" Lawyer

When you hear the word "divorce," you immediately think "lawyer." You need to get good legal advice, but you also need to determine what type of advice and representation you can afford. The problem many women face is that they just don't have the money to get the legal representation they want. Legal aid through your community may or may not be available, but it's worth looking into. Be prepared to spend time waiting in line and filling out endless forms. Free legal aid is reserved for people in the lowest income bracket. Most local courthouses have a self-help center with the legal documents necessary for divorce. Many times, there is a lawyer on staff who can answer basic questions for a nominal fee. If you are not satisfied with what your community offers but can't afford to hire an attorney through the whole process, you can pay for legal advice by the hour as you need it.

Reality checks:

- Don't assume that your husband will be responsible for all of your attorney fees. You might each be responsible for your own, and depending on your financial situation, you might be held responsible for his legal fees. Attorney expenses can also be taken off the top of your marital estate before dividing everything up. Pick your battles wisely because more fighting means less money for both of you and for your children's future.

- Don't expect a judge to be sympathetic and protect you from the big bad world.
- The actual process of divorce can be as short as one month when things are agreeable, or it can drag on for years with acrimonious battles and expenses. It all depends on the complexity of your case, the willingness to work out issues and the state you live in. Some states have a four-year wait list for a couple to have their day in court. Furthermore, there are some states that are called "fault states." That means you have to prove there is a reason for divorce such as adultery, abuse or separation for a certain time before you are eligible to ask for a divorce.

Laura—39 years old

I needed to get out of my marriage but was frightened to make my move. We didn't have a lot of money, and I knew I needed legal advice on child custody issues. My husband knew I was thinking about divorce and would try to convince me that he would get our money and custody of our children. I was frightened and started doing research at the library and reading up on the laws in my state that governed divorce. Some of the information was helpful, but most of it was confusing.

A friend suggested I go for a few free consultations with a local attorney to see if I could find out more. Most of the appointments were sales pitches, but I did get some good general information. I still needed specific details and an attorney I felt comfortable with. On a friend's recommendation, I paid a well-respected lawyer a fee for an hour consultation. By that point I was educated and organized enough to ask important questions. I felt comfortable with him and explained my financial situation. He suggested that I do as much of the work on my own as I could, and when I needed guidance, I should come in and pay by the hour.

I found a great attorney I could count on to help me get through my divorce. I listened to his advice and made my own decisions as I watched the clock so I didn't go over my personal budget. I could finally move forward with a plan and some good advice. I no longer let my husband bully me because I understood the law and how things would likely play out if we went to trial. I was able to get through my divorce mostly on my own, with a lawyer a phone call away when I needed advice. I used my time with him wisely. It worked out to be a few hours of billable time, which I was happy to pay because it empowered me with knowledge that helped me gain my freedom.

Lessons Learned

- There are ways to get good legal advice without paying a fortune.
- You have to be an active participant in your divorce and, when working with an attorney, remember that you are in charge.

Roxanne—28 years old

When we decided to get divorced, my husband and I had been married for five years. We had no children together and had always kept our money separate. We agreed to work out our own details without lawyers and keep the divorce simple. We went to the court-house and obtained paperwork for something called a simple disso-lution of marriage. We took the forms home and filled out our own information to questions such as marital debt, marital assets, our address, length of time we were married, our incomes and so on.

There were lawyers at the courthouse to help with paperwork and any questions before the divorce hearing. They charged $15.00 for fifteen minutes. I spent an hour with one on my own to make sure I filled out the paperwork correctly and that I was not doing anything that was not in my best interest. It was the best money I could have spent for my peace of mind and protection. After getting my questions answered, we were put on the schedule for a judge to grant us a divorce for the price of $263.00.

My husband and I appeared before the judge, who asked us questions regarding our one asset, our home. He asked to confirm if we had sold it and split the profits from the sale. He asked a few more questions to confirm our answers on the paperwork we had filled out. Within fifteen minutes we went from being married to divorced, and I walked out of the courthouse alone.

That was the last time I saw my ex. We talked on the phone a couple of times to tie up some loose ends, but that was it. Preparing for my wedding day was more work than getting my divorce. It was simple, and it was over. I was free to start my new life and find my happiness.

Lessons Learned

- Even in the most amicable and uncomplicated divorces, get-ting some form of legal advice is necessary to make sure you are protected.

- A lawyer will guide you through a legal world that is constantly changing. They will examine your issues, explain your rights and help you make choices that can greatly impact your future.

Finding and Working with the Right Lawyer

If you can afford it and have significant issues, having a lawyer handle your entire case can be the best scenario. There are so many things to consider when choosing your legal representation. It's almost like picking a spouse because you'll be spending a decent amount of time with this person. You need to find someone you click with who listens and can be trusted to work in your best interests, not theirs. You need someone smart who has extensive experience in your county's family court system who knows the judges and local attorneys.

Beware of the Sales Pitch

Remember, all divorce lawyers are salespeople. As in every profession, some provide services that are extraordinary while others see you only as money in their pockets. You need to find a person who will tell you how it really is, not what you want to hear. Be wary of attorneys who tell you they can get you a, b and c without providing case law in your state to back up their opinions and statements (case law is the result of past legal cases that establish the current law). Many attorneys see you as dollar signs when you walk into their offices looking like an emotional train wreck. You can be easy prey to their false promises and unrealistic outcomes.

Make sure you interview a few attorneys and compare their opinions as to how they view your case and how they think it might play out. Ask them for the best- and worst-case scenarios, and beware of someone who promises you the moon and stars. Hire an experienced divorce attorney in your area who specializes in family law and has a good reputation. You don't want a high profile guy from another town who doesn't know the quirks of the local judges and other lawyers—plus you don't want to pay more for their travel expenses.

Asking friends, family and even your therapist for a good divorce lawyer is a good place to start your search. If you can't find an attorney through a referral, you can always turn to the Yellow Pages. Try to interview three before making a decision. Some will charge initial consultation fees while some will give you ten to twenty minutes of their time with no charge.

My interview process included two attorneys who had reputations of being pit bulls. I didn't want to hire them but met with them just to create a conflict of interest in case my husband tried to hire them. While there was no guarantee the attorneys would take his case, it gave me peace of mind that they would unlikely be involved in our divorce.

Meeting with these two guys turned out to be quite entertaining. I found that these two hot-shot lawyers were well known in the legal community but past their prime. The first guy was very old, eccentric and a bit scary. He sat behind his big wooden desk with his pet Chihuahua in his arms. He split his attention between French kissing his dog and listening to my saga. Although he didn't come out and say the exact words, his strategy was basically: crush, kill and destroy. While I had moments that I would have loved to sic this guy on my husband, the moments of sanity helped me realize it would just be a lot of expensive, unproductive bloodshed.

My second interview was with a handsome, tall attorney who had quite the stage presence as he stood up to greet me behind his massive mahogany desk. After walking through his office, it appeared to function like a small factory filled with many employees scampering about at a frantic pace. During our conversation, I found out that he himself was on his third divorce and had three children, all from different marriages. As I sat there in his office admiring his beautiful antiques and furnishings, it was clear that this guy was now content to show up at work to be the window dressing. Most of our conversation revolved around the big cases he defended in the past that resulted in women getting lifetime alimony.

I asked him who would be handling most of the work in my case and he rattled off at least three names. I looked surprised, but he tried to reassure me that he would be representing me if my case went to trial. He then added that his associates did all the pretrial work and would simply fill him in on the details before my day in court. I thought, *Great; the empty suit shows up at court to defend my life and will simply try to wing it.*

After some further conversation, I started to get a strange vibe that he was flirting with me because his questions started getting a bit too personal for a first interview. I became anxious at the end of our meeting when he winked at me and told me he was going to waive his $400 fee as a special favor to me. He hoped I would allow him to help me. I smiled and said good-bye as a little voice inside me said, *Run, don't walk.*

Interview Questions

Remember, you're the boss looking to hire somebody who will work for you. It's not just about feeling comfortable with someone; they also have to be qualified to handle your case. Here are some questions that will help you decide who is most qualified to represent you.

- "How do you describe yourself as a lawyer?" This is open-ended and will give you an idea if he is more trial or settlement oriented, what his experience is, his credentials and how confident he is.
- "How busy are you?" You want to know who will be doing the work and keeping an eye on your case. Will he be answering your phone calls, and how long will it take for him to get back to you?
- "How much do you charge?" Ask him to explain his fee agreement and how he bills. You want to know what kind of paperwork you should see regarding his recorded hours and rates.
- "Who is in charge of final decisions, tactics and objectives?" You need to see if this will be a good partnership for you: Make sure that you will be heard and, ultimately, the one calling the shots.
- "What is your experience in cases with children involved?" If child custody is going to be an issue, ask how much experience the attorney has in this area.

Once you have hired your attorney, make sure of the following:

- Most lawyers have a retainer agreement, which asks for a down payment to be applied to the hours of work that will be spent on your case. The agreement should include the fee schedule of all involved and miscellaneous expenses. Don't sign anything until you fully understand and accept the arrangement. Stay away from nonrefundable retainers that seem too high.
- Your lawyer needs all the facts, so write a complete history of your relationship no matter how ugly, including anything that happened before the marriage. The worst thing you could do is hide something from your attorney that later comes out during trial. The judge will see you as a liar, and, in the end, it may negatively affect your outcome. What you are embarrassed of or fearful about revealing may not even affect your case and probably pales in comparison to other cases they have had.
- Limit your telephone calls and do as much leg work and collecting of information on your own as possible. Most lawyers charge in quarter-hour increments. A five-minute task or call will cost you fifteen minutes, so always make sure it's worth it and don't use your lawyer as your therapist.
- Every time you talk to your lawyer on the phone have pen and paper ready. Prepare for the phone call by writing down your questions and jot down the answers so there is no repetition. Keep a record of the day and time spent on the phone so you can double-check your attorney's monthly bill.

The Lawyer Review

From my own interview process with attorneys and other women's experiences, I have made the following classifications of attorneys:

THE GOOD ONES will work with you and your realistic objectives in the most cost-effective manner. They know the law and have had extensive experience working in your local courthouse with other attorneys and judges. They also have a good track record of success with other people who recommend their services. They will help guide you through the process and offer their support. They take an active role in getting to know the details of your case and guide you through the rough spots of the uncoupling process.

THE BAD ONES are just plain incompetent and unable to help you stand up for your rights. They are disorganized, consistently late for important meetings and don't remember basic facts of your case, for instance, the names of your children. They are constantly handing you over to their paralegals or associates and are unavailable to you until the big money days like depositions and trial.

THE UGLY ONES turn out to be quite competent at their jobs. They know just how to stir the pot to create more chaos and problems, which fuels their billing machine. In the meantime, you get nowhere fast as you watch the money fly out of your pocket and into their deep ones. It becomes a vicious cycle as your spouse has to respond to some of this nonsense, which costs more money, and in the end leaves very little for both of you and your children.

Mental Preparation as You Move Toward Trial

You cannot prevent the birds of sorrow from flying over your head . . . but you CAN prevent them from building nests in your hair.

—Ancient Chinese Proverb

As you move toward trial, I strongly recommend that you start to take care of yourself and slow down. Don't be shy to ask your friends and family for help. It's important to make some down-time for yourself so you can rest your mind and body, which will help you get through this challenging time.

Divorce is a very time-consuming and tedious process, almost like having a second job. You will find yourself with little time to take care of responsibilities in your normal daily routine. Your stress level can be off the charts and your brain can have moments of meltdown. I lost my keys too many times to count, bounced checks, forgot important dates and failed to return important phone calls. For months, my hair fell out in clumps.

My mind was always elsewhere, and I got into some pretty stupid and scary accidents. The first was in my car, pulling out of a school parking lot onto the main road. While looking to my left, before making a right turn, I took my foot off the brake and tapped the car in front of me. Just my luck, it was a brand new Porsche and the guy driving it was the father of one of my son's friends. We pulled over and he refused to get out of the car to see the damages because he was too freaked out. I told him to call me with the damages that seemed minimal. Five hundred dollars and a rental car later, the Porsche was restored to its original splendor. Luckily, the only real damage done was to my checking account. It was my first reminder to slow down.

It's easier said than done, but you have to learn to keep your frazzle factor in check. A quick fix for moments of pure chaos is a simple breathing exercise you can do anywhere, any time. Take three very slow breaths in through the nose and out through the mouth. A chemical reaction takes place as a result of the increased oxygen intake that has a calming effect. Try it now; this simple act can help change your perspective. Learn to feel the frustration and the anger and then let it go. You'll be more effective when dealing with the business of divorce to help get you a good result when you are calm and in control of your emotions. Don't forget to count your blessings every day and make the conscious effort to take a negative and turn it into a positive.

The Legal Process of Divorce

As you enter the divorce zone, the key is to remember that while you can't control your soon-to-be ex, you do have total control over your own actions and reactions through this challenging process. If your husband's being uncooperative and dishonest, you can make a conscious choice to keep your cool and remain an adult. Regardless of the end result, you'll feel better about yourself as you start your new life knowing you presented your case with honesty and integrity and did your best to not waste precious time and money.

Pretrial

Petition for Dissolution of Marriage

The "petition for dissolution of marriage" is a pretty fancy term for papers that state you want a divorce and the things you want once the marriage is over. The papers are filed at your local courthouse with the appropriate filing fee. You can do this on your own or through an attorney. Once you file, the next step is to serve the papers to your husband through an independent third party called a process server.

> If you are the one initiating the divorce, think about your timing and how your spouse will react when you begin the process of serving him papers. If there is a history of domestic violence, or you are afraid your spouse will cause you physical harm, talk to an attorney about a possible restraining order and emergency temporary relief, discussed later in the chapter.

I felt sick about serving my ex. No matter how I planned it, nothing would have made it easy. In the end I chose to serve him at our house first thing in the morning, after telling him the night before. He was upset because I told him at the last minute and should have done it at work. I explained I didn't want him to stress about it all weekend, and it would be too embarrassing to do it at work. In the end, I think he would admit that although it was miserable, it was the best way to have done it.

Funny thing, I expected to feel relief because it was finally done; instead the finality of it all was suddenly very real and painful. The packet of papers seemed to take on a life of their own as they scream out, "Yes, it's happening, you are getting a divorce. This is the end of the promises and dreams for your happily ever after together." No matter how prepared you think you are and regardless of who initiates the divorce, serving the papers can be one of the most trying moments in the process.

Response to Petition and Possible Counter Petition

Whoever is served with the papers is the party responsible for responding to the demands made by the spouse. If the party does not respond, it is understood that the demands are acceptable and a final judgment, with the relief requested in the petition, can be ordered.

If the second party responds to the original petition for dissolution of marriage, they are also allowed to file a counter petition. This is a document that states their demands to resolve the issues of divorce. Both petitions have equal weight in the courts, regardless of who was served first.

Temporary Relief

This is a routine and common way to govern behavior of both spouses during the divorce process. When there is an abusive or dangerous situation going on in the household, you can ask the courts for emergency relief. This is done mainly to protect children in danger. Because the time from filing papers to the actual divorce can take as little as a few weeks to as long as a few years, there must be a temporary agreement. This is a set of rules enforced to determine who stays in the marital home, how two separate homes will be paid for, child visitation schedules, spousal support, child support, property seizure and the restriction of monetary accounts.

The terms and conditions of a temporary agreement/order may set the terms of the final judgment, especially when it comes to child visitation schedules and possible spousal support. This agreement is important because it may be a deciding factor in determining your final outcome.

Discovery

This is the process used by both sides to gather information that will help present their case and substantiate their demands for settlement. It can be the most costly and time-consuming part of the entire divorce, depending on how cooperative you and your husband are in sharing the necessary information. Remember, it's in your and your husband's best interest to cooperate with each other. The first part of discovery requires filling out a financial affidavit.

FINANCIAL AFFIDAVIT—This is a document that requires each spouse to disclose their income, expenses, assets and liabilities. The information provided is critical in determining the spouse's and children's needs and the other spouse's ability to pay support. The information in this document also determines the final financial settlement, whether or not you go to trial. Make sure you take your time when filling this out and review your husband's responses. This document is very important.

More Discovery

If either of you don't cooperate during the discovery process, or questions need more thorough answers, lawyers use the following procedures to collect information:

PRODUCTION—Certain financial documents and information are asked for and are exchanged between parties.

INTERROGATORIES—This is the most common form of discovery. It requires you to answer questions on paper while you are under oath. Most states have standard questions that each side must respond to; however, additional questions may be asked depending on each case.

DEPOSITION—The deposition is when the big bucks start flying out of your pocket. This discovery procedure takes place when production and interrogatories still leave too many unanswered questions and inconsistencies in the information provided. A deposition is an interrogation by the opposing attorney of a spouse under oath with a court reporter recording every word. It can be stressful and there are a few things to consider before going behind closed doors.

During depositions:

- Always be honest. If you do lie, when the truth comes out—and it will—you will be seen as a liar, and it will negatively impact your outcome with the court.
- Only answer the question being asked. Give brief answers and don't volunteer information. If the opposition needs more information, let them ask you another question. If you don't know the answer to a question, say so.
- The other side could be using deposition to see what type of witness you will be on the stand. Do your best to control your emotions. They could be deposing you just to find your weakness for trial, so try not to let them see you sweat.
- After each question, take a moment before answering and breathe or take a sip of water. This will give you a moment to think about your response and your attorney a chance to object if he feels the line of questioning is improper.
- If the deposition goes poorly, consider it practice for your big day in court; don't beat yourself up too much. Review with your attorney how you can be a better witness.

I got my ass kicked in deposition. I had some preparation by my attorney the day before, but my nerves and ego got the best of me. My husband's attorney set me up nicely by being kind and flattering. I was Little Red Riding Hood getting schmoozed by the Big Bad Wolf; I just didn't know it at the time.

When he asked me questions, I gave him more information than I needed to and started to answer questions he hadn't even asked me. I thought I was being helpful to my own case and to the process. It didn't register when my attorney kicked me under the table that I needed to shut the hell up. I let my guard down and just kept talking and talking until I found myself in a deep, dark hole. My husband's attorney went in for the kill as I watched my husband smirking in his chair. Everything that came out of my mouth was now potentially going to be used against me in court. They had a strategy planned that could only work if I handed them answers in a certain way during the deposition on a silver platter, which of course I did with my big mouth.

When the deposition was over, my attorney and I walked out quietly. When we were alone, he looked at me in disbelief and asked what had happened to the cool, calm girl he knew. He explained that I was baited and trapped to say exactly what my spouse and attorney wanted me to say. I felt like I had been plucked and hung out to dry. I went home and fell asleep for twelve hours only to wake up completely exhausted. The day was a lesson that taught me what not to do in court.

The Trial Docket

Your attorney will need to put your case on a list requesting your day in court to resolve your issues and have your divorce finalized. Some states have a waiting list of a few months, while other states can make you wait a few years. While you might not want to go to trial and may think getting your date is premature, put it on the calendar. You can always settle your case prior to the date without having to use the trial date. Just set the date to move the process and your life forward.

Negotiating to Reach Settlement Out of Court

At any time, the case can be settled without going to court. It can happen as soon as the divorce papers are served or at the last minute on the courthouse steps.

- **MEDIATION**—As part of the legal process, you and your spouse will be required to sit down with a trained, objective third party called a mediator. You may do this with or without an attorney, but legal representation is advised if possible. A mediator will listen to your issues and try to help you make a settlement and avoid a trial.
- **FRIEND OR FAMILY MEMBER**—Sometimes someone you know can step in and be the voice of reason and help the two of you reach a compromise you can both live with.
- **KITCHEN TABLE TALK**—If the two of you are on civil terms and have no history of emotional or physical abuse, you may be able to come to terms on a settlement agreement on your own. You want to go into your negotiations fully armed with knowledge gained from competent legal advice and the ability to stand up for yourself. The last thing you want to do is negotiate against yourself. If you feel like this is a possibility, let somebody else stand up for you and be your voice.

The Benefits of Negotiation and Mediation

If at all possible, negotiations and sharing information with your spouse should start at the kitchen table. By using negotiation as a strategy to resolve your issues, you and your spouse stay in control of your final outcome and minimize your expenses of having to go to court.

Some people are better negotiators than others, and I was my own worst enemy. I couldn't think straight, the whole situation was uncomfortable, and I just wanted the misery to end. When trying to resolve issues with my ex I would listen to his side. When it was my turn to respond, I had this incredible inability to objectively argue back with the facts. My emotional stress over the situation was turning my brain to mush, and I allowed him to run circles around me.

Unfortunately, my mediation was a nightmare—our attorneys did not get along and we all had a bad attitude. The mediator worked for the court and was inexperienced. Both lawyers walked all over him, and the process was a complete waste of time and attorneys' fees.

Lessons Learned

- Mediation can work with a strong mediator and all parties coming in with the right attitude.
- Rather than using the court's mediator, spend the extra money and hire a private mediator who is a retired judge or lawyer who has worked in your family court. They have the experience with the law and how it will likely impact the demands both parties are making, which will get both of you more realistic. More important, they can handle difficult situations and keep the process of mediation moving along to hopefully reach some, if not all, resolutions. While it may cost more, it can be worth every cent if you make progress.

In mediation, you can hopefully work out the details of parenting, property and financial support. If successful, pen will be put to paper for an agreement, and the lawyers will prepare the legal documents to complete the divorce. The key is to not walk out of the room until some agreement has been reached. Even if you can resolve some issues and have some agreement on facts, also called stipulations, it will allow the trial to go more smoothly.

In the end, negotiation is a compromise with no winners or losers. A successful mediation results in a resolution where each party feels like they gave something up but overall there is a sense of fairness.

The Trial

- **OPENING STATEMENTS BY BOTH ATTORNEYS**—Each attorney has an opportunity to explain how they are going to present their case and why their demands should be granted. The attorney for the spouse who filed initially is first to present his case.

- **DIRECT EXAMINATION**—The testimony starts with an attorney asking a witness questions; you will likely be one of the first. This is one of the most stressful parts about going to trial. The questioning typically starts with the person who files, the petitioner or plaintiff. The first few questions get you used to testifying and include basic information like your name, age, address and employer. Then your attorney will guide you through a line of questioning you have already prepared for and discussed. If there are some facts about your marriage that make you feel uncomfortable, you should be the one who introduces them rather than your spouse. You will be able to talk about it from your perspective and possibly soften the impact. When answering questions don't look at the attorney, look at the judge. He or she is the one who needs to understand the situation and the facts. The attorneys already know everything.

Okay, your direct examination has gone well. Just when you were starting to get comfortable, you realize that when your lawyer is done, it's time to face:

- **CROSS-EXAMINATION**—This examination is performed by your spouse's attorney, the bulldog. This is the time to take a few slow breaths and drink some water. You need to think on your feet, be ready for anything, and under all circumstances don't lose your cool. You should be respectful and do your best to answer the questions. If you don't understand the question, tell the attorney you don't and he will try to rephrase it. Don't answer any questions you don't understand. If the attorney asks more than one question at a time, you can kindly ask him to ask you one at a time because it is confusing you. The lawyer will try to ask you questions that require only a yes or no answer. If you tell the judge that it's difficult to answer the question with a yes or no, he may or may not allow you to explain further. If he does not allow you to or if you are unhappy with your responses, your lawyer will give you a chance to explain during:
- **REDIRECT EXAMINATION**—After cross-examination your attorney

will give you a chance to recover from any damage or confusion that might have happened during cross-examination.

The other side goes through the same procedure, and in the end there will be closing statements by each attorney and a final opinion by the judge. Most of the time there will be a written decision received by mail, which can take weeks or months and can be very nerve-racking. Once in a while, a judge may rule from the bench and tie up the details in a written formal opinion.

The Big Day—Humans Judging Humans

You have been preparing and biting your nails for the big day, and now your court date is here. By this time, your attorney will have prepared you for trial and you should have a pretty good idea about what your day will look like. You should have been advised on how to act, how to answer questions, and how to dress.

Depending on the complexity of your case, a typical trial will last two days. The actual day typically starts with a 9:30 to noon session with a fifteen-minute break in between. Court goes back in session at 2 P.M. and runs until 4:30 P.M. with a fifteen-minute afternoon break. If you do the math, you will be paying your attorney for eight hours while you only get about four hours of actual trial time.

A few tips:

- Wear professional clothing and shoes. Don't forget hose or matching socks, the judge has a good eyeshot of your legs under the table. You want to be respectful to the court and the judge but comfortable because you will be there all day.
- Do not bring food in the courtroom or chew gum. Water should be provided at your desk.
- No cleavage and keep the jewelry down to a bare minimum.
- Limit the amount of people that come to court to support you, but

have the ones you need. You don't want it to look like you have your entire bridesmaid entourage with you. You can't have people sit in the courtroom with you if they are going to be witnesses.

- Make sure whoever comes to court can control themselves if they hear something from the opposition they don't like. The judge will frown on any verbal and nonverbal commentary.
- Remember that when someone comes to court to support you, they are getting a bird's eye view of your entire financial and emotional personal history.
- Only in extreme cases are children asked to come to the court to testify. The courts are making great efforts to protect children from the stress and potential emotional damage that can be created by having a front row seat at their parents' battle.
- It's not just what you say, but how you say it and the nonverbal communication that the judge will watch and listen for.
- Even if your spouse's attorney tries to push you over the edge, keep your cool. A judge wants to hear answers that are truthful and to the point.
- Address the judge as "Your Honor" or "Judge." Do not talk to him unless you are addressed. If you are asked a question, make eye contact and answer the question effectively.
- Do not snarl at your spouse. Keep your reactions genuine but under control. If the judge sees disrespect or hostility, it may discredit your testimony.
- If your spouse is the plaintiff, his attorney might make a bulldog move by calling you as the first witness. The sole purpose of doing this is to try and unnerve you; relax because you saw it coming.
- Make sure you use an extra-strength antiperspirant each day you go to court; don't ever let them see you sweat. If you need a bathroom break or a glass of water to regain your composure, take it.
- DON'T EVER ARGUE WITH THE JUDGE.
- Don't try to act smarter than your spouse's attorney; you will be sliced and diced. Sarcastic remarks might make you think you are winning the battle, but they will only help you to lose the war.
- Talk slowly and pause before answering a question. It will give

your attorney time to object if necessary and will help the court reporter to get everything down.

- When your husband is testifying under direct examination, have a pad and pen ready. If he says something you disagree with, write it down so you don't disturb your attorney from listening to his testimony. You will be able to confer with him before your attorney goes for cross-examination.
- Keep in mind that while your spouse is testifying, the judge will be watching you. As mentioned earlier, judges pay close attention to verbal and nonverbal communication. Don't hiss, make crazy faces or blurt out that he is lying. Keep your reactions genuine without overreacting.

Reality in the Halls of Justice

Here are a few highlights of divorce court many women have shared with me. It will help explain why all of the rules, laws and regulations of the family court can be overridden by what I call the human factor.

- You have been a homemaker and mother for the last twelve years, and you are asking for significant lifetime alimony. You find out that the judge who is hearing your case is a woman who is divorced herself with two small children and works over forty hours a week. She has a reputation for being unsympathetic and hard on women in your situation.
- There is a history of domestic violence in your marriage. As you walk in the judge is clearly unprepared for your case. He tells you what a shame it is that you can't work it out because you are such a nice-looking couple.
- You learn that your attorney and your soon-to-be ex's attorney don't get along. During the process of depositions and possible negotiations, they get into a fistfight. Not only do you have a ringside seat, you're paying a premium price to watch it all happen while nothing constructive gets done except more legal fees for your attorneys.

- You become friendly with your attorney, first mistake. He asks you out on a date. You gracefully decline his offer, explaining you would like to keep your relationship strictly professional. He accepts your explanation, but now you feel like you are walking a tightrope. Months later he starts dating another client only to have his heart broken. You find yourself nursing his broken heart in the middle of a deadline he must meet for your case. While you want to switch attorneys, you realize the deadline gives you no time to start fresh with someone new. You are trapped like a rat.

- In the middle of your preparation for going to trial, your attorney informs you that he is running for judge. He asks if you would host a lunch to help get him votes and then stand outside the voting polls to hand out his flyers. He is focused on winning a seat on the bench, and you realize your case is at the bottom of his list of priorities. You now have to change attorneys and start all over again.

- No matter what you say, your attorney is habitually late. There is a mediation scheduled to try and resolve issues and avoid a trial. You find yourself standing in the courthouse waiting again for a man you are paying a fortune to. Your spouse and his bulldog attorney are aggravated by the inconvenience and are starting to give you the evil eye as you stand there completely alone.

- After all your time, money and preparation for your day in court, you watch the judge's eyes glaze over. His head is propped up in his hand and his feet are stretched out on the bench. You realize that it's not your imagination that he is fast asleep and snoring during your sworn testimony.

- Your ex lied his ass off during deposition, which gives you a good idea of what he will do during the trial. Friends who could come forward in your defense either come up with excuses or disappear from sight. You realize your ex has gotten to them somehow, and now it feels like you're in the middle of a bad Mafia movie. Your whole case rides on "he says/she says" and who the judge believes. Your outcome depends on whether or not your judge can sift through the bullshit and see the truth.

- Your constitution is tested during trial when your ex's attorney verbally attacks you. He comes at you with red cheeks, barking questions at you as his spit flies in your face. All of his sentences start with "Isn't it true," followed by a complete lie. Hopefully, you find your quiet happy place and remain calm and unmoved by his bully scare tactic. The song "Who Let the Dogs Out" comes to mind as you hope your judge will call him off. You have to try to keep your composure as you answer his questions with the truth. You learn to counter his "Isn't it true," with "That's completely incorrect."

- For two years, you have been asking your attorney for the deed to your house you got in a final judgment involving equitable distribution. He tells you that he would have to go to court to get it. He reassures you that your ex will eventually get it to you because legally he has to, so why waste the money? Two years pass and an appeal looks like it's on the horizon. You panic and tell your attorney to go get the deed to the house and he assures you 100 percent by law, he will walk out with it. The call comes and he tells you he didn't get the deed. He's never seen a judge make a decision like that, but, ultimately, he has the right to do what he wants. So much for what the law and procedure say, not to mention your lawyer's 100 percent guarantee.

- You got snookered by an attorney who was too much of a salesman. He made promises about your situation that were not possible within the scope of the law. He painted an unrealistic picture just to get your business and reach into your deep pockets. You took the bait because he told you what you wanted to hear. You dug your heels in for what you believe you were entitled to. Your spouse had a similar type of attorney who was not realistic about the situation. Both of you bought the sales pitch which resulted in years of costly, nasty litigation. In the end, you both realized that with the right attorneys, you could have settled out of court in mediation.

The Ruling: Reaction and Reflections

The end of the day was drawing near and things were wrapping up at my trial. After over a year of preparation and enormous expense, it was time for the judge's almighty ruling. While both attorneys were making their closing statements, an urgent call came in for the judge. His daughter just gave birth. He could not wait to get out of the courtroom. He quickly summed up the case and his decision. I had an out-of-body experience. He was talking about numbers for alimony and child support. He was talking about taxes, net and gross, and I was lost. His voice faded into a distant muffled sound and all I could really hear was the sound of the air conditioning going on and off. He was literally disrobing and walking out the door as the attorneys practically begged him to sort out the final details. His response was that we should settle it over a beer. A BEER! I felt like I was in a bad cartoon where all of the voices and sounds were distorted and muffled. After a year of preparation, and the price of two college educations in attorney and accountant fees, did he really say we should talk about it over a drink? In a flash, the black robe was gone and it was over. A strange silence hung over the courtroom as we all tried to figure out what had happened. It was like a hit and run.

As I stood there in my confusion, my family and friends gathered around. Everyone was blurting out questions trying to make sense of the ruling. It was absolute mayhem; even my attorney looked shell-shocked. My husband, who was now my official ex, walked out of the courtroom. My attorney asked everyone but my dad to leave as he tried to interpret the judge's ruling.

As everyone left, I sat down quietly at the table, and out of nowhere, I turned into an uncontrollable sobbing heap. I had held it together for over a year and the last two days were a pressure cooker. It all came to a head in a cathartic release of pent-up anxiety and energy that was held at bay for way too long. For about five minutes, I was inconsolable as my dad and my attorney sat by me and let me get it out of my system. I eventually went from full sobbing to uncontrollable laughter. The whole damn bloody mess was over, or so I thought.

My attorney took me out for a glass of wine to explain what the ruling meant and to celebrate that it was over. It was the first time I think he did not charge me, but I can't be sure. I was spent and had a terrible headache. All I wanted to do was go home and hibernate in my bed so I could come back to life again. I felt like I lost on a lot of my issues, and I felt enormous disappointment and disbelief. Once the dust settled, I decided to live with what the judge ruled on the bench, and I was grateful it was over. Unfortunately, we were not done. We had to go back for several rehearings. Each attorney interpreted the loosely held together final opinion differently. Several thousand dollars later, the judgment was made final, but two years later I would find myself back in the court system for something called an appeal.

If one party is not happy with the decision and can prove that the judge abused his discretion, the entire case could get overturned and you would go for another trial. Months after the appellant hearing, word came in the mail that the whole case was overturned. I would be spending the next two years in the court system with a brand new judge and trial—unbelievable! Don't worry; this rarely happens because most people never even make it inside a courtroom for a trial, let alone to an appeal. The whole thing was absurd.

My ex and I decided to stop making our attorneys rich and finally settled matters out of court. I think we both walked away feeling that we gave much up, but the silver lining was that we were done. I could finally exhale, and a wave of relief washed over my body. After three years of anxiety, attorney's fees and fear of the unknown, I felt like I had some closure.

Looking back at the whole experience, there were many things I think both of us would have done differently regarding our divorce. Our bank accounts and our emotional well-being took quite the beating for way too long. After having some time away from the whole ordeal, I was able to laugh as I looked back on my courtroom experience and the whole "trauma drama" of it all.

If there was a highlight of the trial for me, it would be my husband's attorney cross-examining me. As I mentioned earlier, I had been destroyed during my deposition. Well, practice makes perfect. Having learned my lesson, when it really counted in court, I used my mouth intelligently. I was ready for my husband's attorney and all of his tricks when it really mattered.

I had this bizarre sense of calm, and his bulldog schtick was no longer scary but almost comical. I was able to deflate almost every attack. This time, when he came at me with his three questions in one sentence, I didn't go into verbal diarrhea mode. I started off my response respectfully telling him to please ask one question at a time because I really did want to give him answers but he was confusing me. He was annoyed and flustered after the judge agreed with me and told him to take it easy on me.

His grilling lost momentum once he had to ask one question at a time. My answers were short and to the point. I turned out to be an excellent witness after all. I watched the frustration on my husband's face as his attorney tried everything to get me to say or act a certain way, but I was a rock and answered to their detriment and my benefit. This time around, I was prepared and kicked some major ass when it counted. In the end, I got some serious S-A-T-I-S-F-A-C-T-I-O-N.

The hard part for me was over and now it was my husband's turn in the hot seat for testimony and cross-exam. It was entertaining for a while, but then I got annoyed at his response to some questions. Apparently, I was making faces and hissing noises in response to what was being said because my attorney told me to chill out. He told me to start writing on my legal pad any relevant information he might need or to just write and look interested but unmoved by the testimony.

I retreated and tried to find my happy, quiet place. I started using a chant I learned in meditation class that says, "I am blissful, I am immortal." It made the whole courtroom thing seem like a bad play I was watching from a distance. I started to write the chant down, and before I knew it, I had three pages of it and my spouse's attorney was done with his little tirade. After that, I started to realize how ridiculous the whole thing was and I was done with feeling anxious. I did everything I could do to increase my chances of a good outcome and then I let it go until the process was over, and I survived very nicely.

Looking back at my trial, the journey was challenging and required a lot of preparation and a cool head. It's very serious business, but through it all you have to remember to breathe and laugh. Regardless of the outcome, you will find a way to make your new life work. Once you get past your legal divorce, it's time to relax and focus on your emotional recovery.

The Growing Pains of Divorce

Now that you're finishing up your legal divorce, it's time to come to terms with your new reality. I never truly understood or could relate to my single friends who complained of living in a "couple society" until I became single myself. I found the social aspects of divorce and uncoupling to be challenging, but there were many things that made my transition into single life easier.

There is a whole network of divorced people that the newly divorced can tap into once you know what's out there. This demographic is rapidly growing, and a whole industry has been created to cater to their needs. For instance, there is now something called a "certified divorce planner." This is a new profession that has been created to help couples divide their assets and plan hip rituals like the "divorce shower" and the "unwedding" where couples give their rings back and ask each other for forgiveness. There are support groups out there for the single parent, children of divorce, divorced and dating, recently divorced and blended families, and the list goes on.

Divorce and Death

Some people compare the grieving process of divorce to the death of a loved one. Both scenarios share similarities but have differences in how individuals and society treat someone dealing with the trauma of losing someone they once loved. Many people facing a divorce find themselves soul-searching and asking similar questions to those who have recently faced the death of a loved one: What is this all about? Who am I and where am I going now that they are gone? The difference is that the divorced person can face a lack of support and sympathy compared to someone mourning a death.

Kerry—34 years old

I knew my husband for ten years, and we had been married for the last seven. Our relationship was solid until his job started to require that he travel a few times during the month. It started feeling like a long-distance relationship and we grew apart. When we did spend time together, all we did was fight. Pretty soon we couldn't even look at each other; I wanted to see a therapist but he just wanted out.

Within a year, we were divorced and I found myself alone and devastated. I had lost my best friend and lover. At first my friends were wonderful and supportive, but they quickly lost their patience with me. They said I should just get over it and move on with my life, he wasn't right for me and I'll find someone better. Blah, blah, blah, who were they kidding? I had considered this man my soul mate and he just walked out of my life without try- ing to save our marriage. I felt worthless and lost. Nobody under- stood what I was going through, and I was all alone in my misery.

I started to look for something to make me feel better so I turned to my personal vices, S&S—shopping and sex. I was swiping my credit card so much that the numbers on it started to wear down. At the end of the month, I had a few quick fixes that involved jewelry, sexy shoes that I could never walk in and a dresser filled with Victoria's Secret lingerie and nobody to play with. Along with that came a credit card bill that gave me a serious "I'm in debt up to my eyeballs" headache. I decided to self-medicate with sex and started sleeping around.

It wasn't so much the sex but the human touch that I craved and some validation that I was desirable. I went out all the time just to avoid coming home to an empty apartment where I felt nothing but pain and loneliness. Eventually the sex got old, and I had worn every piece of lingerie I owned. The whole thing just stopped feeling good.

I retreated to my bedroom and spent nights crying my eyes out into my pillow. I realized that I had to stop running from my feelings and just deal with them. I allowed myself to stay in bed in my pajamas all weekend. The only time I got up was to eat or go to the bathroom. Eventually I saw a therapist for a few months and worked through my feelings of anger, confusion, sadness and betrayal. It took some time, but I finally started to enjoy life again and feel like myself.

In therapy, I started to analyze the process I went through to get over the trauma of my divorce. I hated to admit it, but I think it would have been easier for me if my husband had died. I'm cringing as I say that, but I would not have felt so betrayed, and knowing he was never coming back would have forced me to let him go. If I had been widowed, friends and family would have come to my house to console me after the funeral. They would have stopped by with casseroles and food to last me for weeks. There would have been plenty of sympathy and I would have been nurtured and taken care of. I would have participated in all

*of the rituals that come with someone's death and been able to let
go a little easier, maybe.*

*When I got divorced, I walked out of the courthouse alone,
feeling devastated. A judge gave his approval for the divorce, and
the day seemed to go on, unnoticed as my dreams were nullified
by a piece of paper signed and stamped by a total stranger. To the
rest of the world, it was just another day. I grabbed some lunch
at a drive-thru and went back to work. Friends and family
tapped me on the shoulder and told me to have a stiff upper lip.
That was my day when my marriage died.*

Lessons Learned

- Just like in death, a divorced person needs to go through
  the grieving process. You can't hide from it; to get over
  it you have to really experience the loss of that person's
  scent, companionship, understanding and friendship.
- Hiding the grief with diversions and denials only
  prolongs the inevitable pain you have to experience in
  order to move on.

There Is No Switzerland in Divorce

Telling close friends and family can be cathartic. You no longer have
to maintain the façade of being the happy-happy couple. You are free
to be honest about how miserable you have been; suddenly you can
exhale and breathe easier. It's like that saying, "The truth shall set you
free!" If you are the one who initiates divorce, friends and family will
react differently, depending on how much they knew of what was going
on in the marriage. Possible scenarios include:

- A sigh of relief as they ask you why it took so long.
- Shock and disbelief with acceptance.
- Shock, disgust and disbelief that you would even consider divorce.
- Expected the breakup and want you to find your happiness.

Regardless of who ends the marriage, some family and friends may start off neutral but ultimately choose sides. Even with their best intentions, staying neutral or loyal to both of you is impossible; there will be a natural progression toward the person with whom they share a stronger emotional bond.

Prepare yourself because it's human nature to judge others and take sides. You will feel like you are under a magnifying glass before, during and after the actual divorce. The breakup of your marriage has caused a disruption in the status quo of your social structure; some people need to place blame for the unwelcome change. Others will judge you to make themselves feel better about their own misery or to justify their own marital existence. It's almost a feeling that says how dare you break away from the pack on your own and leave us here. Some of it is jealousy that you had the courage to do it, while others feel vulnerable because if it happened to you it could happen to them. Some married friends will treat you as if you have a contagious disease called "the divorce bug."

Unfortunately, these reactions only intensify the feelings of loss that each divorcing person must face. Already feeling alone and vulnerable from the breakup makes you more anxious about losing more. Many times, both spouses will start to compete for the sympathy card in hopes of maintaining their friendships, and it can get ugly.

Some people may conveniently forget that you were miserable for the last ten years while they watched your spouse treat you poorly. While they understand why you left your husband, you will be left in the dust as they tend to the wounded party. As soon as friends and family see your husband looking like a hurt puppy dog, they will rush in for the rescue with invitations to dinner and movies on the weekends. Suddenly, poof, you are out of the picture.

There are a few other breakup scenarios that have predictable

outcomes when it comes to your friends and family dividing the camp
into his side and her side:

Infidelity and the Curse of the Scarlet Letter

If a man or woman dumped an unsuspecting spouse for another partner, it's a sure bet that at first the friends will rally around the spouse who
was cheated on and snarl at the adulterer. During the competition for the
sympathy card, the expanded version of the truth will come out in the
form of "he says/she says." Judgment day comes after mutual friends
listen and draw their own conclusions of who deserves what. True friends
will stick by your side regardless of the situation; the rest will fall by the
wayside.

*α*lexis—36 years old

*When news got out that my husband and I were getting
divorced because I had been unfaithful, many mutual friends
dropped me like a hot potato while others slowly faded away. My
ex and I had a troubled marriage for years, and ultimately I
found comfort in someone else's arms.*

*I was prepared for my husband's guy friends to hate me, but I
didn't expect to lose some of my girlfriends. To my surprise, a
close friend was very angry with me, she felt betrayed and caught
in the middle. Her husband was friendly with my husband in our
comfortable little social circle that I just turned upside down. She
was hurt that I kept my affair a secret and then scolded me for
having sex with another man. She followed with a monologue
about marriage being worth the hard work, and you just can't be
a quitter.*

*After arguing and feeling like I had to defend myself, which
was ridiculous, we settled on agreeing to disagree. Within two
months we had nothing in common to talk about and our*

relationship faded away. Her married life was too different from my new single status and she wanted no part of it. Just like that, a girl I had known for years and whom I thought I could always count on disappeared from my life, along with most of my old circle of married friends. I felt like I lived through two divorces, one from my husband and the other from my friends, which was quite unexpected.

Lessons Learned

- Divorce with adultery can play itself out with the old double standard. When a woman cheats she may be looked down upon and cast off. If the man strays, he is just a victim of his primitive nature and biology. Many times the woman wears the scarlet letter and the man will be forgiven for most of his sins.

Mutiny—Choosing to Fly Solo

Marriages sometimes break up simply because one or both parties decide that it simply doesn't work anymore and they want to move on. Family and friends can be supportive of your decision and praise you for your courage, or they can get downright hostile and tell you that you're nuts and making the biggest mistake of your life.

Angie—41 years old

I was married for twenty years, and the last ten had been a struggle. The process of trying to make it work was draining the life out of me. I was in a relationship that was neglectful and mentally abusive; our house was filled with animosity and disappointment. My husband seemed to function just fine as he made a separate life for himself with friends and activities that did not include me. One day I finally decided I needed to get out of the marriage and start a new life for myself.

My friends and family had seen me suffer with depression and physical ailments over the years as they watched a confident young girl turn into an insecure, sad woman. They tried to intervene and show my husband what he was doing to me and how he was tearing our marriage apart, but their efforts were useless.

I finally reached my limit and found the courage to leave my husband. I was nervous about telling my family because they are very religious and don't believe in divorce. I thought they might have a hard time with my decision but would accept what I had to do. I met more resistance than I ever expected, which only made my transition into single life more difficult. To make matters worse, my husband was shocked and out of his mind that I had the nerve to leave him. He did a great job playing the anger/sympathy card and rallied friends and family in his corner.

I suddenly felt like I was in the twilight zone. It seemed that everyone had been brainwashed and forgot how horribly my husband treated me. They actually tried to convince me to go back; after all, he didn't want a divorce. Of course he didn't, he enjoyed all of the benefits of being married: sex when he wanted, home-cooked meals, housekeeping and a wife who contributed to the household expenses. They were persistent and argued that marriage isn't perfect; I should be grateful that he didn't use drugs (suddenly alcohol isn't a drug), sleep around, gamble our money away or hit me. So what if he ignored me and verbally abused me, I should be grateful for what I had and go back with him before he changed his mind. Now I felt like I was living in the Dark Ages. I had a mental image of a caveman dragging a woman across the ground by her hair while she had a forced smile on her face.

I listened to my gut and divorced him anyway. It was easy to lose him but not the friends and family who divorced me from their lives. My choice to declare mutiny and jump my ship of miserable matrimony was more than they could handle. I think many of them couldn't stand to watch me do something they were too afraid to do for themselves.

Lessons Learned

- You have to be strong enough to listen to your gut. Nobody knows you better than you know yourself.
- Don't make life decisions to please others, do what works for you.

Divorce Etiquette: Is There Stationery for Divorce Announcements?

How and when you tell people can be difficult and painful because it feels like you are telling the world you failed at marriage. On top of that, you have to deal with reactions and questions from family and friends on what is a very personal matter. People announce their news depending on their audience. One woman I interviewed told her disapproving parents by writing them a letter. She explained that her decision was made and trying to talk her out of it would create a wedge in their relationship. She said that while her parents weren't happy, the letter lessened the blow, and when they had their first meeting she was happily surprised to feel their acceptance and support.

Another woman worked in the same building as her soon-to-be ex. They used to be known as a happy couple, but her co-workers were sensing unrest and started asking questions. Realizing she could no longer avoid the inevitable, she sent an e-mail around the office. It simply stated that she was getting a divorce and she would appreciate everyone's respect for her privacy about the matter. She said she was grateful for the concern but did not want to discuss it and to please continue to treat her like they always had.

Other people choose not to tell anyone because they feel it's too personal and no one's business. I couldn't agree more—you owe no explanations. Just be prepared for inquiring minds and "the gossip mill." If you do choose to answer questions, keep it short and sweet without bad-mouthing your spouse. Here are just a few situations you might have to deal with:

- People you hardly know will get in your face and ask, "So what happened?" Some people will be sincere and offer genuine sympathy, while others are just trying to get a juicy piece of gossip. It can be intrusive and at times shocking. Prepare yourself so when it does happen you'll have a planned response that is polite but stops their interrogation. The key is to throw a question back at them that makes them uncomfortable. My favorite thing to fire back was: "It was all for the best. So how are things going in your marriage?" If done correctly, it sounds semipolite but stops people dead in their tracks. For the truly obnoxious, you need to come out and tell them that they are making you feel uncomfortable and it's simply none of their business.

- As soon as people heard about my divorce, I had neighbors calling me and saying, "I'm sorry to hear about your divorce. By the way I heard you were selling your house and I have someone who wants to buy it." I never had the slightest intention or said a word about selling my house. Even better were the inquiries about my ex just weeks after our official breakup: "I hope you don't mind, but I would love to set my friend up with your ex if that's okay with you?" I felt like I was that woman on her deathbed in *Zorba the Greek*. All of the friends and family were waiting by her bedside for her to die so they could be the first to ransack the house. I wanted to ask these people if they were brain-dead or had been raised by bears! Somebody should start a class: Divorce Etiquette 101.

- When you meet new people and they find out you are divorced, they feel comfortable dumping their marital problems on you. Suddenly you have unwillingly become their divorce therapist because you have lived through the ordeal.
- A girlfriend tells you that she ran into an old acquaintance of yours. This woman heard through the grapevine that you kicked your husband out of the house and asked for a divorce after you found out he had been sleeping with a stripper. It was an ugly divorce and you are still in court trying to get rid of him. You are now engaged to be married to a man with four small children who desperately need a mother. The real story: Your marriage broke up because you grew apart and it was an amicable divorce. The two of you are still friends and call each other to see how things are going. You are now dating a man for the last six months who is wonderful and has three grown children.

Transitioning—I Love Him, I Hate Him, I'm Nuts!

A divorcing woman told me she was feeling intense hate and anger toward her spouse. She actually fantasized over plans that plotted his demise with at least three disastrous endings. She looked at me and said she thought she was losing her mind because while she hated him during the daylight hours, she was having mad, passionate sex with him in her dreams at night.

I tried not to laugh because I had experienced a similar emotional roller-coaster ride but was now past that stage and had some perspective. All of these crazy emotions, feelings and dreams are NORMAL! The way to successfully get through this time is to acknowledge you are not crazy, just perfectly human. You can love someone and hate them at the same time, want to have sex with them but choose not to be with them. You are not a bad person for thinking or feeling a certain way as long as you don't act on something you will regret later.

Anger is an important emotion you will experience as you come to terms with the end of your marriage and try to let go of your old life. The trick is not to get stuck with this emotion for too long or let it control your actions. To get off your emotional roller-coaster ride, you must own all of your feelings and allow yourself time to grieve and feel the pain. Let them out by writing about them, crying about them or just plain screaming your head off. Give yourself permission to spend time with your feelings so you can eventually let them go and move on. Try to use your anger in a positive way to make some much-needed changes in your life.

Here are a few helpful tips:

- Don't let friends and family rush you through your process. While you don't want to stagnate in misery, it will take time to recover from divorce. At your own pace, deal with your loss and all of the crazy emotions.
- Use this opportunity to learn more about yourself. Go to the bookstore and get lost in the self-help section. Pamper yourself with a massage, a walk in the park or a movie. Do something that you didn't think of doing when you were married, like a new hobby or sport. Now is the time to nurture yourself back to life.
- Ask for help from others who can relate and empathize with your situation. Friends, family, religious counselors or therapists can all help you through your mourning process. Make a conscious effort to focus on the positive.

After dealing with legal issues and carving out a place in your new life, you probably feel like you've been forced to run on empty with no relief in sight. You are probably struggling with a lot of emotional issues and just have not had a chance to deal with yourself yet. Things will start to calm down and you'll have time to put some energy into your emotional recovery.

Your Emotional Divorce and Recovery

The Caterpillar

Living through the emotional and financial chaos of divorce makes you feel like hibernating in your bed until next spring. You have been running on adrenaline for too long and your entire body hurts; all you want to do is collapse. While you've been locked away in your marital death grip, the rest of the world has continued at its usual pace. It's finally time to return to the land of the living. The problem is that when you look in the mirror, you don't feel great about the person looking back at you.

I felt fried after the entire process and referred to myself as the "crispy critter." During a particularly stressful day, I had taken my children to a place called Butterfly World, a sanctuary where they cultivate and study butterflies in a greenhouse. We learned about the caterpillar, a worm-like creature that crawls slowly through its world. I definitely identified with this primitive life-form. During its life cycle, it creates a chrysalis, where the caterpillar cocoons itself for a few weeks. That sounded like the cave I was looking for to hibernate in. While hiding away from the world, an incredible metamorphosis takes place, changing the crawling caterpillar into a beautiful flying butterfly.

From that day on, I visualized myself on a similar journey—I was going to make myself over from the inside out. After some alone time, I would emerge into the world transformed and take flight. I stopped feeling sorry for myself because I now had a mission to accomplish. I wanted more than just a new hairstyle and a buff body. I wanted to fix what was hurt inside while I worked on my outside package.

My spirit and self-esteem were crying out for resuscitation, how would I find the energy for my metamorphosis? I remembered the story of the little engine that could. Whenever I felt like I was running on empty, I would chant to myself, *I think I can, I think I can . . . I know I can, I know I can,* until I reclaimed my life. There was a lot of work ahead, and the first thing that was screaming out for help was my self-esteem.

Dealing with "The Divorce Hangover"

Now that the legal battle is over, you probably feel like one of the walking wounded. You have a document in your hands that says you are legally divorced. Your marriage is over, but you still feel strangely attached to it. Instead of being tied to your former spouse, you're tied to the emotional aftermath of your divorce. You're probably feeling a bit lost as you ask yourself, "Who am I and how did I get here?"

While you felt some relief knowing that the business of divorce was finished, you thought you would feel much better than you do. You are sick of feeling the heaviness of your heart and the weight of the world on your shoulders. The papers say you are a free woman, but you feel imprisoned by your anger, depression and anxiety about the future. It feels like you have been holding your breath under water—you want to break to the surface and breathe again.

There will be many things you have absolutely no control over as you move forward, but you do control your attitude and perception as you travel through this part of your journey toward recovery. Your success will be determined by the state of mind you choose every day when you wake up. Now is a critical time to look inside yourself and figure out who you are and what you want in your life. It's important and helpful to surround yourself with people who love and encourage you, but ultimately you are going to be the one who rescues yourself.

The first step toward getting your "emotional divorce" is to surrender to the process and accept that you are now divorced. You can experience rage, depression and manic happiness all in an hour. Relax. Some of these crazy and painful feelings are a normal part of the healing process. Achieving your emotional divorce requires you to understand and experience your feelings in order to move into the next stage of healing. The next few pages will explain the gamut of emotions you will likely experience as you move toward your emotional recovery.

Anger

Anger is such a normal human emotion. How quickly you heal depends on how long you stay with your anger and where you put the energy once you let it go. I have a clear memory of a session with my therapist when she told me it was time to stop complaining about my ex and get a handle on my anger. She said I was giving it too much power and control over my life. My assignment was to go home and write down all my negative feelings toward him; then when I was done, take the papers and throw them out. What a waste—I wanted to mail him the papers. But she told me how ridiculous that would be because it would only make him happy to know how crazy he was making me.

I followed her advice, but instead of throwing away the papers, I decided to burn them. When no one was around, I had a little cremation ceremony. Surprisingly, it was very satisfying. That simple burning ceremony helped me to feel and acknowledge my anger and then let it go, as the papers turned to ashes and floated into thin air. I felt a sense of peace, and was able to let go and move on. That's not to say I still don't have issues with my ex. He is still a big part of my life because we are raising two kids and there are times we butt heads. Our old issues and behaviors can rear their ugly heads, and I still feel the anger well up inside of me until my blood boils. The difference is that I make a choice not to marinate and fester in it too long because it's not healthy for me or our kids.

When my intense anger was gone, I was able to think more clearly. Now I had time to look at my experience and learn from it. Stepping away from it helped me to get some insight and perspective of what went wrong. I was able to look at my own part for the breakup and take responsibility for my actions. Part of my problem was all of those fairy tales I grew up with. I had this notion that Prince Charming would come into my life and sweep me off my feet. We would ride off into the sunset together and live "happily ever after." Yeah, right!

My distorted sense of relationships and marriage gave me little responsibility toward my own happiness. I depended on my husband to make me happy; it was so ridiculous because I gave up my power voluntarily. Rather than getting mad at myself, I was going to learn not to make the same mistakes again. A girlfriend of mine once told me that you have to be the ice cream sundae and a man is just the cherry on top that makes it a little sweeter.

I felt empowered because I realized I controlled my destiny; it wasn't dependent on someone else. More important, I was able to learn about myself from my divorce experience and identify what my soul required in a relationship. What looks good on paper doesn't always work out so well in real life. My new checklist is completely different from my checklist of a decade ago, now that I have grown up in the real world.

Resentment

Holding on to anger for too long creates resentment. Holding on to resentment will only continue your nightmare and cause you to become embittered. It can consume your life because you are so filled up with it that there is little room left for anything positive to come into your world.

Resentment is usually experienced by the unwilling partner in the divorce. For some people, holding on to anger and resentment serves a purpose. It helps them hold on to the relationship because they believe a bad relationship is better than no relationship at all. Resentment is a big road block that can detour your healing. Do your best to recognize it and then let it go because you are only hurting yourself.

Resentment is like taking poison
and waiting for the other person to die.

—Malachy McCourt

Guilt

Guilt is a common emotion people wrestle with in divorce. The "Dumpers" beat themselves up for hurting a spouse who wanted to stay married. The "Dumpees" feel guilty because they think they should have done more to keep the marriage together and prevent their partner from wanting out. Guilt is a punishing emotion that can freeze up your emotional process toward healing. Professional counseling can help you accept yourself and your new situation so you can move forward and learn from the experience of being human.

Failure

It's hard for people to deal with the fact that they have failed at their marriage. Many are left with "I could have, should have, would have." The reality is that failure is an unavoidable, healthy and necessary part of life if you want to grow. Take the word "failure" and start to define it as "opportunity."

After my legal battle started to wind down I remembered a book I read in college by Ernest Hemingway called *A Farewell to Arms*. It was about World War I, which I felt like I had just lived through. There was a great line in the book that I always carried with me that seemed most appropriate for this chapter in my life. Hemingway wrote, "The world breaks everyone and afterward many are strong at the broken places."

When it comes to divorce, are you the person who allows the circumstance to destroy you, or will you become "stronger in the broken places"? Failing in your marriage isn't what matters, it's how you bounce back. True success in life comes from many failures.

Depression

Depression affects people differently, and it can depend on who initiated the divorce. Most often it has a greater impact on the "Dumpee" who has to deal with a crashing self-esteem. When the reality of divorce hits them, they are not equipped to handle the transition and they may slip into a major depression.

Moving through depression is usually a necessary and natural progression toward recovery. Without it you would not be able to get through the many emotions that finally give way to grief, mourning your loss and eventually forgiveness. Depression becomes problematic if you withdraw into yourself and away from others for too long. If you think you are suffering from serious depression, seek professional help now.

Denise—31 years old

When my marriage broke up I lost my husband, my high school sweetheart, my best friend, my only lover and my comrade through a significant part of my life. To add to my torture, we actually dated after our divorce even though I knew he was seeing "the other woman." I didn't care because I was so desperate for his love and attention and I was sure he would eventually come to his senses and return to me.

We spent weekends together but during the week he would disappear and I would not hear from him at all. For a while I convinced myself that I could make do with the crumbs he threw my way, but soon I realized I was being used. The sex wasn't good enough to repair the gaping wound he created every time he disappeared. He would jump back into my life and rip my heart out just when I was starting to get myself together again. I felt like I was living in a "somebody done somebody wrong song." I couldn't handle it anymore and put an end to the vicious cycle. I knew I did the right thing, but it felt as though I had cut off my right arm. I was miserable and my self-esteem was at an all-time low.

After cutting the ties with my ex, the impact of the divorce hit me head on. I felt so ashamed that he cheated on me and felt that everyone was laughing at me for not knowing how long he had been unfaithful. I felt like the clueless wife who was the last to know of her husband's infidelity. Of course, nobody was laughing and not many people knew, it was just the hell I created in my own mind.

The next few months I fell into a depression and flirted with paranoia and something called agoraphobia, a fear of leaving the house. I had gone from living a social life with friends and family to a life as a hermit. It started slowly and escalated to the point where I wouldn't even get out of my bed to eat. Every night after work and every weekend I would spend alone locked up in my apartment. Friends would call to meet for dinner or a movie, and I would tell them I was too tired. Their calls continued, but I would let the machine pick up and never bothered to return their calls.

First I would come home and have dinner in front of the TV. Then I would come home and immediately change into my pajamas to have dinner in front of the TV. It progressed to dinner in my PJs while I ate in my bed. Soon after that I lost my appetite and went straight to bed and wouldn't get out unless it was to use the bathroom. My body just shut down, and I slept all the time. This was my way of not having to deal with my life and all of the emotions that were swirling around my head. I lost ten pounds in less than two weeks and started to realize I had a problem. I literally felt as if I were drowning.

My mother insisted I get my ass out of bed and see a therapist. I refused; I had sunk so deep I didn't know if I could swim to the top and I was afraid. She broke into my apartment, opened all the windows and stripped the sheets from my bed while I was still laying in it. I'm still not so sure how she did that. She refused to leave until I promised that I would get some help and get out of the house. It wasn't easy but I found a good therapist and returned to the land of the living after a few weeks.

In therapy I started dealing with the emotions I escaped from by sleeping all the time. My counselor suggested that I should use some of my alone time to start journaling. I took her advice, and it was that process that helped save me from myself. While I didn't want to talk to many people, I found it very helpful to talk to myself by pouring my fears and feelings out on paper. I would entertain myself by creating stories with different scenarios of how I would get back at my ex for cheating on me and treating me so badly. My favorite story was when he came knocking at my door pleading with me to take him back. He would complain about his girlfriend and tell me what a mistake he made and how much he loved me. I would laugh at him and give him the "I told you so," then take him back just so I could torture him for the rest of his life.

I spent a year in therapy, read books and took a few self-help seminars. My self-esteem was better than ever and I was starting to enjoy single life and had started dating. Funny how life works out, my ex did come back asking for my forgiveness and asked if I would take him back. It was so surreal, and to my surprise, I felt nothing. There was no desire to rub his face in it like I fantasized. I took a good hard look at him and was free at last from the power he had had over me all of those years. I was no longer in love and no longer wanted him in my life.

It was a defining moment. Instead of my very rehearsed, "I told you so," I simply said thank you, but no thank you. His mouth dropped open in disbelief, and I almost laughed because I realized I was no longer his emotional hostage. In that moment in my mind, I forgave him for being such a shit and forgave myself for taking it for so long. There was no magic pill in my recovery. It required time, a therapist's guidance and my own hard work. I was finally able to let go of my past and move into my future.

Lessons Learned

- "You can't run and you can't hide from your problems." You have to deal with your new situation and jump back into life again, even if you start with baby steps. People in your social network can help you get through your nightmare of divorce if you let them. Don't shut them out of your world, try to return calls and make plans to go out even if you don't want to.
- There are many ways people can learn to improve their attitudes and perspective that will ultimately improve their lives. It's a matter of moving forward and not allowing yourself to get stuck in your own muck. Doing things for yourself like seeing a therapist or taking a meditation course can empower you to get out of bed in the morning and face the new day.

Euphoria

That's right. In the middle of all of these crazy emotions that don't make you feel good, there will be moments of euphoria. Whether or not you were the Dumper or Dumpee, there can be moments of relief and a feeling of freedom. You are no longer rotting in an unhappy marriage, and there is a sense of hope and adventure on the horizon. You realize the legal nightmare is over and now is the time to start with a clean slate of your new life on your terms.

There is definitely reason to feel good because everyone coming out of divorce has a chance at a happier life. The problem is there are so many other difficult emotions to deal with that there will be times you feel like you are playing emotional ping-pong with yourself. Prepare yourself for conflicting emotions that will make you feel like you are losing your marbles. It's all very normal and things will calm down as you work yourself through the process.

Anxiety

Many women experience significant anxiety and fear about their futures. While you are dealing with the emotional loss and adjusting to a new way of life, you have to deal with work, pay the bills and maybe take care of children. Suddenly you are the head of the household, and it feels like the weight of the world is on your shoulders because you realize it's suddenly all up to you. The worst part about anxiety is that it fuels depression, and the more depressed you get, the more anxious you become. It's a crazy cycle that you will experience until you get a handle on managing yourself and your new life—which takes time.

I remember quite a few times breathing into a brown paper bag to keep myself from hyperventilating. As mentioned earlier in the book, I learned a simple breathing exercise that put an end to my hyper episodes. It involves taking deep breaths through the nose and slowly releasing them through your mouth. If you repeat this exercise three to four times, you will notice a calming sensation that takes over your body. This simple exercise changes the chemistry in your body and has a real physiological effect that you can feel immediately. Figure out what works for you. Many women I spoke with said the best way to combat their intense anxiety was to put their sneakers on and run off all their crazy energy.

Most women I spoke with said they were amazed at how well they could get along in life alone once they were able to calm down and focus on what they needed to do. The worst part for them was the fear of economic instability. Once they had a plan of action for their financial survival and actually did something about it, they became less anxious.

Responsibility

In a marriage it takes two to tango. Very rarely is it one person's fault for the breakup of a marriage. If you take responsibility for your part of the breakup and learn from the experience, you'll be closer to achieving a relationship you want in the future. Even if your actions only contributed to a small part of the failed marriage, take responsibility for them. Pointing your finger at someone else is always easier than taking a good hard look at your own issues.

If you truly want to move on and have peace and happiness in your life, choose to learn from your mistakes and failed marriage. Stop wasting your time and energy participating in the blame game; nobody wants to hear it. Use your energy to improve yourself and learn from what you did wrong. If you don't, chances are you'll only repeat the same mistakes in your next relationship.

Once I accepted responsibility for my part in the breakup of the marriage, I started to feel a certain peace. I was able to move to the last and most important stages, sadness and forgiveness.

Sadness

I think once you hit the emotion of sadness, you are close to achieving your emotional divorce. I remember being in therapy trying to articulate some recent feelings and I couldn't come up with the right word. My therapist looked at me and asked if what I might be feeling was sadness.

That was it! I was relieved to have a name for it, and once it was identified I started to cry. After a couple of minutes I felt such relief that I went
from crying to laughing.

I no longer felt hostile toward my ex. I started to empathize with his
loss and emotional journey. This was a man I shared my life with for a
long time, good times and bad. We had met in school, started a chiropractic practice together, survived my bout with cancer and had two
beautiful children. I knew I would always be connected to this man
because of our children. Our shared experiences made him a part of
who I am, like it or not. Hating him would be a waste of energy and
could only be destructive to my well-being as well as our children's.

There were plenty of reasons to be disgusted with each other during
the legal battle, but it was over and our lives were splitting off in different directions. After being hard and angry for so long, I finally soft-
ened and in my heart I wished my former spouse well. I was finally
done with all of my crazy emotions and "trauma drama." I was able to
mourn the death of our marriage and move on with the rest of my life.

Forgiveness

What is your definition of forgiveness? Webster's dictionary defines
it as: "to give up resentment against or the desire to punish; stop being
angry with; to give up all claim to punish or exact penalty." There is definitely a lot of stuff packed into that definition, but in the end it's about
making a choice to let go. The challenge is that not only do you have
to forgive your ex, but, more importantly you have to forgive yourself.

Rochelle—31 years old

*I got divorced from my husband after a year of counseling,
during which we both tried very hard to save our relationship. We
had fallen madly in love with each other a few years earlier and
married shortly after we met. It was an amazing love affair until
we had to settle into the realities of married life.*

A few months after our honeymoon, there was already trouble in paradise. We just couldn't see eye to eye on anything, and we were always fighting. It was clear that we were just not compatible. We had a turbulent few years until we saw a marriage counselor, which made life a little more bearable. The problem was that our relationship only worked when we were in therapy. It became clear to all three of us that our marriage was not going to last; in the end, my husband pulled the plug and I was grateful.

We had an amicable divorce and went our separate ways. I was unexpectedly filled with anger—not toward him but toward myself. In my head, I started to play back a session I had alone with our therapist. We got into a discussion of what I thought I needed from a relationship. I quickly answered laughter, lots of affection and emotional intimacy. He then looked at me with a puzzled expression and asked, "Well then, why did you pick your husband?" He explained that my spouse was not the type of guy to provide me with the things I needed to feel satisfied in a relationship. He made a good point, I rushed into a marriage that wasn't a good match. It was doomed from the beginning because I chose someone whose emotional makeup could never give me the basic things I needed in a marriage.

From that day on I blamed myself for not knowing better and making a mistake we would both suffer for. I started to remember all my doubts about getting married during our short engagement. We had trouble getting along then, but our fights would always end in great sex. It was a vicious cycle and deep in my heart I knew our engagement should have been broken. I was just not brave enough to do it and was caught up in all the passion and romance.

It wasn't until years later that I was finally able to let go of that burden and forgive myself for choosing the wrong partner. It happened after I read the book Getting the Love You Want, *by Harville Hendrix. The author explained that sometimes, unconsciously we pick partners who have similar traits to our parents so we can deal with unfinished business. We feel like we can be with this new person and get some of the things we needed and did not get in our childhood. It made perfect sense to me because I always thought my husband was very similar to my mother. Funny, I seemed to have resolved my issues with my mother once my marriage was over.*

When I learned there are choices we make that are beyond our control because we make them unconsciously, it was easier to forgive myself. I also realized how young and inexperienced I was at that time compared to where I am now. My ex and I were just doing the best we could under the circumstances. After a year of beating myself up, I found the right book and the right therapist and suddenly I was free. I accept the fact that I am an evolving human who will continue to make mistakes and hopefully learn from them.

Lessons Learned

- Once you forgive, you can let go and open yourself up to more positive energy. Suddenly you start attracting wonderful people into your life as you learn to be more compassionate and patient with yourself and others.
- Therapists are human and therapy is not magic. Therapy can teach you skills and point you in the right direction; ultimately, it's up to you to do the work necessary to achieve your emotional divorce. You have to shop

around to find the right person and approach that is best for your personality. You also have to do other things outside of therapy to help you heal.

Attitude

Through my journey of divorce, I have learned about attitude and how much it affects your life. Many people I interviewed for this book helped me along my journey. Afterward, I was able to put many women in one of two groups. "The Bitters" were people who chose not to learn from their experience and were caught up in the blame game. They seemed to make a choice to stay with their anger and let it consume them. Their perspective on their life and future was filled with negative energy, and they were just miserable characters.

On the other hand, "The Sweets" made a conscious choice to learn from their mistakes and move forward into a new chapter of their lives with a good attitude. They pulled their switch to the "on" mode and viewed their new life with a fresh perspective and energy that helped create their new happiness. When asked what went wrong with their marriage they didn't bad-mouth their ex and they took responsibility for their part of the breakup. It was a pleasure to talk to these people. I found myself attracted to their energy and optimism compared to the negativity of The Bitters, whose company just brought me down. The Bitters would complain about how they couldn't meet anyone and how most of their friends disappeared. After interviewing them, it wasn't hard to understand why they were so alone.

As a student of chiropractic, there was a philosophy I came to know and embrace in my life called the law of universal intelligence. Part of the philosophy was that the more positive energy you put out into the universe, the more positive things will come into your life. Everyone has had a taste of this, some more than others. The best way to describe it is when you feel like you are "in the zone." Maybe it's like a game of tennis when every play you make is incredible and you feel like you can't lose. Or you might remember being out with friends on a Saturday night at a party and everyone wanted to meet you. It's this euphoric feeling that makes you feel golden, and it comes from a place inside that projects this positive energy like a burst of sunshine. Figure out a way to harness your own sunshine.

Self-Esteem

Self-esteem is that deep-down, inside-
the-skin feeling you have of your own self-worth.

—Denis Waitley

The work on self-esteem has been used to create shows like *The Oprah Winfrey Show* and *Dr. Phil*. The book stores are packed with information on how to feel good about yourself. It's a great topic to discuss because your success in life is determined by your self-esteem. After divorce, low self-esteem is a very common problem because you are walking away from something you failed at. This feeling of low self-worth can cause depression, insecurity and low confidence. It's like having a voice inside that is always disapproving.

You will be facing many new challenges now that you are divorced. Having a low self-esteem will only cause you to stumble and feel overwhelmed as you attempt to create your new life. It's time to rebuild your confidence and self-esteem. The first step is to improve your attitude and change the voice inside your head. Change the negative chitchat to a conversation that speaks only positive and inspiring thoughts and remember:

"We are what we think."

Here are some suggestions to help you improve your self-esteem. Remember that everyone struggles at different times with their confidence and self-worth; it's all part of the human experience and all very workable.

FACE YOUR FEAR—There are so many things you can worry about and question when you divorce. Common questions are: Will I ever stop having feelings for my ex? How will I make a living? Will I ever find somebody to love me? and How will I take care of my children? If you face your fears you realize they are manageable, and once you start working out a plan to make your new life work, you will feel more confident.

LET GO OF THE PAST AND PERFECTION—Mistakes are an opportunity to create a better future. Thinking about what you could have done is a waste of time and energy because you can't change what happened, so let it go. Human beings are not supposed to be perfect; in fact, most people find perfectionists unattractive and difficult to be around. Our imperfections are what make us beautiful; your self-esteem will grow when you accept yourself for exactly who you are.

FOCUS ON YOUR STRENGTHS—Start making lists of things that you are good at and the compliments that others have given you. Accept your limitations and focus on putting your energy into what you can do well.

FEEL SUCCESS—Think about the person you want to be and what you want to achieve. Don't be afraid to ask for what you want and celebrate when you get it. You deserve it. Set yourself up for success by taking on projects that stretch your abilities but have a high likelihood of success. Set goals for yourself that are realistic and always work and grow toward your potential.

STOP PROCRASTINATING—Getting bogged down with "stuff" only produces anxiety and worry. Set daily goals for things that you need to do, it will give you a feeling of accomplishment and success. Your self-esteem will improve and your worries will be fewer when you see yourself moving in a positive direction.

POSITIVE INTERACTIONS—Hang out with positive people who bring out the best in you. Do something nice for someone else. It will make you feel good and boost your self-esteem and prevent you from getting too self-absorbed.

After recovering from your "divorce hangover" with a healthy self-esteem, you will realize all the possibilities that are open to you as you create your new life on your own terms.

Taming Your Inner and Outer Monsters

My opinion of myself still wavers from time to time when I hear someone making negative comments. It's easy to feel good about yourself when people are telling you how wonderful you are; the true test is how well you stand up when people and circumstances pour out negative energy toward you. I have come to accept that I am a work in progress who gets better as time moves on, but it isn't always easy. When I get stuck, I always go back and reread a book that always gets me back on track: *The Four Agreements,* by Don Miguel Ruiz. It's a fast read that can give you some inner peace and change how you see the world.

The key to a truly healthy self-esteem is maintaining that good opinion of yourself regardless of what others say and feel about you. It can be quite the challenge when you are riding the roller-coaster of divorce. Whether you like it or not, people will judge you as you start your new life. Start developing a thicker skin because regardless of the situation, you will always have people who will be disapproving and unable to maintain a relationship with you.

I remember thinking about Superman and his weakness, kryptonite. The only way he could stay strong was to stay away from it. That's how I started viewing people in my life who were throwing out negative energy; I just stayed away. If that vision didn't work, I would think of the bloodsuckers as vampires. In my imagination, I would surround myself with garlic to repel the evil monsters. I found myself being very entertained by my thoughts. Instead of feeling down about myself and crying, I laughed and felt good.

Use your imagination to conjure up anything that might help you deal with the negative publicity. Most important, keep your sense of humor and remember to laugh. The most likely reason people judge and gossip about you is because they are miserable in their own lives. Keep the chant in your head: *It's not about me, it's about them.* Instead of feeling anger, feel compassion for those who are so miserable they get joy out of putting other people down.

Inevitably, you will re-evaluate your friendships once the dust has settled after your divorce. Surround yourself with people who will love and support you through your transition. Having friends and family around you who will listen to your occasional ranting and raving sessions can be the most important part of maintaining your sanity. If you are alone, joining a support group can also be helpful. Check your paper or religious organization for any divorce recovery programs in your area. The Internet can also be a good referral source. You'll be able to share and connect to others going through similar circumstances and learn how they overcame their problems.

Makeover Time: Mind, Body, Spirit

It's time to take charge of your life on your own terms, NOW! Take some quality alone-time to figure out who you are after your divorce and what you now want out of your life.

Only when one is connected to one's own core is one connected to others, I am beginning to discover. And, for me, the core, the inner spring, can best be refound through solitude.

—Anne Morrow Lindbergh, *Gift from the Sea*

I love the Anne Lindbergh quote, but it doesn't mean you should start living your life like a hermit. Do things for yourself that make you feel good, like hanging out with friends, window shopping, going for a bike ride, getting a massage or just taking a walk in a park. Distractions like these are good because they will help recharge your battery and stop you from getting completely consumed by dealing with "your stuff."

During my divorce, I felt as if I was on pure adrenaline most of my days, stressed out to the max. I was in a constant state of *frazzle,* and it started to take its toll on my health. My wake-up call came when a patient asked if I was all right because I had lost so much weight. I looked in the mirror and got on the scale. I had turned into Twiggy overnight! I also started to count how many times I had been sick over the last few months. My body was drained and I was going downhill. It was time I took my own advice; I started my own personal journey toward healing my mind, body and spirit.

Your Personal Odyssey

Think of this time as your own personal odyssey where you get to make yourself over from the inside out. It's a time to reconnect to your inner soul and heal your spirit. You have a chance to learn more about yourself and your past mistakes as you let your forgiveness set you free.

Divorce can be an excellent opportunity to bounce back into a life that is more fulfilling than you ever imagined. The process you go through requires you to draw on your deepest reserves. It can push you to the edge, teetering over a deep abyss, but instead you realize you can soar like an eagle. Do you want to fall or fly?

You can start tomorrow with a clean slate and a positive attitude, or you can choose to wallow in the past and maintain your miserable status quo. It's up to you because you have ownership over your life and the freedom to choose your attitude every day you wake up. Actions or inactions will determine the course and level of happiness in your life. Life beyond divorce requires you to take several steps out of your predictable box as you make your way into a new life. If you stretch yourself to grow and learn from your experience, you will be more likely to succeed in finding love again, but most important, you will love yourself.

Spirit: Lost and Found

My first steps to reclaim my spirit were to search for different ways I could feed my soul. The hardest part was starting, but once I took the first steps, I developed a game plan to help my heart learn to sing again. I spent hours in the bookstore and sat with any self-help book I could get my hands on. The one thing I always wanted to do was learn to meditate. Through the Internet I found a wonderful center in my neighborhood that provided many different types of unconventional healing including meditation. The teachers there helped me develop a whole new way of thinking and looking at the world in my everyday life. It makes a big difference in my quality of life, how I feel and how I interact with others.

When you think about your divorce, remember that saying, "When one door closes, a window opens." You might miss some of these windows if you are not in a healthy state of mind. There are many ways to heal your soul and find your spirit; it's a matter of finding what works for you. There are conventional and unconventional therapies that can help you on your way toward recovery. If you are a skeptic, take this time in your life to open your mind and consider one of the following ways to help you find your spirit and reclaim your life.

Conventional Therapy

The most widely used conventional treatment for depression as a result of divorce is psychological counseling. At times antidepressants are prescribed by a doctor that can be used in conjunction with counseling. These options of treatment can be highly effective when you find the right doctor to work with.

I started treatment years before my divorce. I met some very interesting therapists who could have used some time in the chair themselves. As a doctor, I understood that the fancy degree on the wall does not change the fact that the person behind the title is still very human.

One woman told me she remembered going to therapy to save her marriage. She started getting the feeling that the therapist had a crush on her husband, but she let it go, thinking it was just in her head. After their marriage ended in divorce, she found out that the two of them were in a hot and heavy relationship. Yes, it sounds like it should only happen in the movies, but occasionally crazy things like this do happen in real life.

The reason I mention this is that you have to listen to your gut when you are seeking help from any health care professional. As a chiropractor I have interacted with many different physicians to help give the best care to my patients, and I've realized all doctors are just like anybody else in a profession—some are good, some are bad and some are just plain nuts. Make your own opinion and remember the fancy coat and degrees don't mean anything if you are not comfortable with the person and the care you are receiving. Find someone you are comfortable with who has good credentials and recommendations; otherwise, you will be wasting your time and money.

It took three different therapists until I really clicked with someone. I didn't need somebody to massage my ego or tell me what I wanted to hear, I needed a highly qualified doctor I could relate to. I spent a few sessions with two different doctors and learned things that were helpful but felt after a few sessions it was time to move on. Once I found the right therapist, she played a huge role toward my road to recovery. She was able to tap into me in a way that opened my heart and released my negative energy. It was the beginning of my recovery; years later, I still see her when I need a psychological tune up.

Medication

As a chiropractor, I believe in finding alternatives to medications because of their negative side effects. I have always believed that medications are to be used only as a last resort when nothing else seems to ease physical or psychological pain. With that said, going through divorce can result in severe depression and anxiety where doctor-prescribed medication can be your best option.

Keep in mind, everyone has a unique body chemistry and different reaction to medication. It requires patience to find the right medicine and dosage, and you must allow a few weeks for it to get into your system to work. Talk to your doctor about your depression and let him make recommendations you can consider. Severe depression can be a steep downward spiral. Don't wait to make the call—get the help before your problems get out of control.

Unconventional Therapy

There are many examples of unconventional therapy that can be used in conjunction with standard treatment. The following treatments have been very helpful to me during my emotional chaos. Consider these a sampling of things to explore that can improve your physical and mental well-being, especially as you journey through your divorce.

Chiropractic

Chiropractors detect and correct something called vertebral sub-luxations. Subluxations are slight misalignments in the spine that can interfere with the nervous system and cause many health problems. Chiropractic is a drug free, noninvasive treatment that uses spinal adjustments to help eliminate nerve interference so the body can function to preserve and restore optimal health.

As a chiropractor, I have personally experienced and seen patients with many symptoms resulting from stress. They can include tension headaches, migraines, back pain, muscle tightness, upset stomach, nervous twitches and more. Chiropractic is helpful because it works to normalize and maximize the functioning of your nervous system by removing the interference caused by a vertebral subluxation.

Think of the nervous system as a hose that supplies water to plants in a garden. If you were to step on the hose and stop the flow of water from reaching the plants, they become weak and start to wilt. When you take your foot off the hose and remove the interference, the plants get what they need, and they remain strong and healthy. Chiropractic offers a natural way to let your body heal itself. Remaining strong and healthy will help you meet the many challenges of divorce and creating a new life.

Mantra Meditation

I'm not talking about a bald yogi sitting in the lotus position chanting weird sounds for hours at a time. The practice I'm talking about can fit into your everyday lifestyle. It can take as little as ten to twenty minutes a day and have substantial benefits toward the quality of your life.

The literal meaning of "mantra" is "to set free from the mind." Mantra meditation gets you to focus on words, phrases or your breath to get the constant drumbeat of worry out of your head. It takes practice and patience but you can reach a peaceful, trancelike state of heightened consciousness and awareness. The benefits are feeling refreshed and positive. You start paying attention to the little wonders in your life, which helps you to minimize the negative.

Going through the stress of divorce and all of the changes I had to deal with, my brain was on overload. I couldn't sleep or rest. There was just no way for me to turn off the worries and thoughts. Mantra meditation was very helpful to clear my mind of the constant static by concentrating on something as simple as my breath or a sound. It was the most challenging skill to learn and the most satisfying.

I relied upon mantra meditation to help keep my sanity through the legal chaos of divorce. I was able to deal with all of the "divorce stuff" without losing my mind. Meditation gave me a calm, deep-down-inside feeling that reassured me that everything was going to work out fine. Once my divorce was final, I was able to use meditation to help me through the hard times as I transitioned into my new life.

In the beginning, I found that I didn't have the discipline to meditate at home without someone leading me. I was more successful with group meditation in a room filled with people who were relaxed and peaceful. When I couldn't get into that special place, I would fall asleep in ten minutes, which was fine because my body needed it. I woke feeling refreshed and at peace. Instead of getting frustrated by my inability to reach that trancelike state, I would remember my teacher's encouraging words. He explained that there were no failed attempts at meditation because each time we tried we would come closer to knowing it. The main ingredient for success was to commit at least ten minutes every day to help make it a habit.

Sometimes I experience a meditative state where an hour feels like a couple of minutes, and it gives me a feeling of calm. By making meditation a daily practice, I find that I am able to effectively deal with the challenges I face. Fewer things bother me, and I become aware of the simple miracles in life. The great thing about meditation is that it benefits you but also everyone around you. My children had a calmer and happier mommy, and my family seemed to tolerate me better because I was a little less nuts. The hard part is making it something that you continue to do. It's like developing the discipline to go to the gym to work out your physical body. This is something you have to do to work out your spiritual body.

A Course in Miracles

A Course in Miracles is a complete self-study spiritual thought system that can be discussed in a group setting. The objective of the work is to undo guilt through forgiveness to achieve universal love and peace as you make God part of your thoughts and daily life. The course is not a religion, but a universal spiritual teaching.

The most important miracle I experienced through this course was a shift in my perception of how I saw my divorce, as well as my world. It helped me to look at a negative in my life and change it to a positive. This new perception helped change my attitude and how I felt about challenges in my life. It also helped me to accept that there are many things in life I have no control over. When I find myself in situations that make me uncomfortable and out of control, I put the problem in God's hands and ask for guidance. The solution eventually presents itself to me, which puts me in a calmer state of mind. By getting in touch with your spirit, you will notice everything in life seems more manageable and less stressful.

If it's not A Course in Miracles, find something to tap into your spirit and soul. It might be religion, nature or just watching your kids play. The key is to be able to step back from the chaos in your life and realize it's just a passing phase. Getting in touch with your spirit will help this crazy time pass through you rather than knocking you off your feet.

(NLP) Neuro-Linguistic Programming

These are simple mental exercises to reprogram thoughts, feelings and actions. By learning about unconscious thought patterns, you can learn different mental and emotional responses to create a positive healing process.

NLP was able to help me get my anger and anxiety under control, which was starting to affect my health. I have used this technique since that time and found it to be very helpful in my life. A therapist taught me there are many emotions that can be uncomfortable to experience even though some serve a purpose. While you can't escape them, there are many ways you can reprogram your mind about how you react to them. You can learn to manage destructive emotions so they don't consume your daily life and well-being.

The first question my therapist asked me was how I viewed my anger. I responded by telling him it was a volcano that was bubbling over with lava, and it was about twelve inches from my face. I was actually very surprised by my own response since it described exactly what was going on in my stomach. Through visualizations and sounds, I was able to take situations where my angry volcano was at full boil and minimize the feeling by changing how I visualized it. I was able to picture the volcano cooling down and moving into the distance as it became smaller and smaller.

Suddenly situations that would normally cause me to be reactive had very little effect on me. I was able to take a step back and handle myself much more effectively. I became an observer of my own emotions and actions of others. It prevented me from having knee-jerk reactions to things I didn't like. Watching and practicing the technique allowed me to choose how I was going to internalize something and respond to it. I was empowered because I realized I was in control of how my emotions would affect me mentally and physically. Once I learned the techniques to cool down my anger, the fire in my stomach fizzled out and I was able to stop popping antacids.

Yoga

I didn't think I would make it through my first class. I was in pretty decent physical shape so I decided to take an advanced class—big mistake. I lost my balance during most of the class and I was ready to give up, but the feeling I had when I was done was amazing. It was like having a runner's high without being so hard on my body. I took a few beginner classes and worked my way into the advanced class and I was hooked. Besides a great workout, it really is a great way to help you find your center through complete concentration. I couldn't think about my divorce if I tried. After each class I felt a combination of calm and euphoria. Learning and mastering new moves gave me a sense of accomplishment that helped me take on more challenges in my daily life. I started to feel this unshakable confidence, and my body felt and looked great.

Butterfly Girl

Remember that caterpillar that wrapped the chrysalis around itself? It hid away from the world to experience a metamorphic miracle that transformed a crawling creature into a beautiful butterfly. That's what your journey is going to be like. The most important part of the transformation was when the caterpillar was on the inside, working alone within the chrysalis. When all of the creature's work was done, she emerged from the old into the new and took flight with her new wings.

Once you have done the work on the inside by nourishing your mind and spirit, it's time to do some work on the outside package. You are a completely different person now, and it's time for you to show it on the outside too. Take your self-esteem up another notch by improving your appearance with something as simple as a new hairstyle or new wardrobe. How you feel on the inside is the most important, but feeling good about how you look can give you extra confidence and a zip in your step. Get yourself physically fit and feel confident with your body. Treat yourself to a makeover or get your eyebrows shaped—just do something different to make you feel good without going too crazy. It doesn't have to be a major change, just try to do something for yourself that will make you feel good and ready to take on the world.

Beauty Alert

We live in a society where a high price is paid for unrealistic beauty. Some women actually believe that plastic surgery is a necessity in life. I know women who made it their business to get the breast implants and Botox injections before or soon after their divorce. Their main game plan was to get primed and primped before returning to the singles scene so they could find a man.

I've had conversations with these women, and they are often miserable regardless of their outside beauty. It was like they were dying on the inside and had this really fancy mask to hide it. I'm all for plastic surgery and doing things that can improve your appearance; however, the beauty you feel inside has to match the outside beauty. If you're not feeling good from within, improvements of your outward appearance will only take you so far. Most people will tell you that the most attractive quality a person can have is confidence. That comes with a healthy self-esteem which needs constant tweaking and a spirit and soul that needs constant nourishment.

With that said, it's still important to maintain yourself, even when you are living alone. A friend of mine was telling me that she didn't even bother shaving anymore because there was nobody around to impress. The hair on her legs was so long it felt like a soft layer of fur that kept her warm at night. One day she took a full frontal look at her body and was horrified at what was going on around her bikini area. She said she felt like she had turned into a beast, a manly beast. That was all she needed to wax, shave and trim up that special area. Now it was about pleasing herself and how she felt underneath her clothes. She bought some Victoria's Secret panties and some matching bras to finish her look, and she was feeling like her old hot self again. When she walked down the street, it made her feel sexy. It was her own little secret she kept from the world as she strutted her stuff.

I learned how to do my makeup differently, waxed my eyebrows, changed the color of my hair and let it grow long. I felt great and some people were shocked at how well divorce seemed to be agreeing with me. I didn't feel like my physical features changed that drastically. I just felt like my glow came from the inside out with the help of a few blonde streaks around my face. I was feeling good about myself. I had made a choice to get out of my depression and work toward my recovery. The outer package improvements were an added bonus compared to the extreme makeover I did on my self-esteem.

Tips for Butterfly Girl

- It's not so much your outward beauty, body or age but how you work your entire package that helps you to take flight.
- Take the time you need to regroup but don't forget to be a social butterfly with people who support and love you. Don't hide yourself away from the world for too long. Learn to balance alone time and social time so you can enjoy your days. Life is short, so go out there and smell and dance among the beautiful flowers.
- Older butterflies can still fly with grace and beauty. If you haven't heard, sixty is now the new thirty thanks to babes like Lauren Hutton. Demi Moore and Kim Basinger have done wonders for women in their forties and fifties. We can start courting young males straight out of the chrysalis without even a flutter.
- After the storm, a butterfly always knows that the sun will come out and provide everything she needs if she just searches and works to get what she wants.

Adjusting to the Minutiae of Single Life

Butterfly girl has new wings as she learns to fly solo in her new world, but there will be some growing pains along the way. The separation before and after the actual divorce can be a combination of relief, sadness and pain wrapped up in one messy package. After living with someone for years, there are things you take for granted and just get used to having around. When that person is suddenly gone from your environment, it can be a bit of a shock when the sense of loss kicks in. Even the person who initiated the divorce will struggle with the transition. It can be as significant as an empty bed or as minute as a missing toothbrush.

Here is a list to help you prepare for moments of expected and unexpected grief. Focus on the positive and the things that can be gained from the change in your circumstances as you learn to reframe your new life.

Loss—Having a warm body sleeping next to you.

GAIN—Absence of snoring and the ability to sleep diagonally across the bed if you wish. Set up an environment for the perfect night's sleep.

If you are desperate for something to hold on to, buy a body pillow. It's softer and more flexible than the real thing.

LOSS—The empty side of the sink in the bathroom, closets, drawers, nightstands and so on.

GAIN—Are you kidding me? It's time to spread out and go shopping for some nice new decorative tchotchkes!

LOSS—That background noise of ESPN or sports on the television that let you know he was close by.

GAIN—Again, are you kidding? Go out and buy some Enya and fill the house with music or start enjoying the Lifetime and Oxygen channels.

LOSS—The scent of the man.

GAIN—It doesn't always smell so good. Go out and buy some aromatic candles and incense to create a relaxing environment that pleasures your senses.

LOSS—Not having someone to share meals with.

GAIN—The good news is that you don't always have to prepare dinner. If you want to eat cereal and fruit for dinner, nobody is complaining. Watching TV while you eat dinner can be very relaxing and you get sole possession of the remote.

LOSS—Not having someone to do the handy work around the house like fixing the toilet when it overflows.

GAIN—This can be a challenge. Once you start doing things like this for yourself, it gives you a great sense of empowerment. I am woman, hear me roar. If not, hire a cute handyman who can service your household needs and look good while doing it.

LOSS—Having companionship and someone to go out with on Saturday nights, special occasions and vacations.

GAIN—You have a chance to expand your horizons by stepping out of your box. You will be forced to meet new people, which can lead to new experiences and new adventures. This also frees you up to hang out more with your girlfriends.

Loss—Sex (but how good was it anyway?).

GAIN—There are some amazing technological advances in the latest hardware for women! Buzzzzzzzz.

Loss—The dream.

GAIN—If you take the time and allow yourself to grieve and feel the pain of losing the dream, you can move on to create a better one. Many people have come out of divorce saying that it gave them an opportunity to look at themselves and their lives honestly and make some positive changes that have helped to enrich their lives and increase their happiness.

SPECIAL NOTE—There will be moments of vulnerability that will intensify feelings of loss, such as wedding anniversaries, birthdays, holidays and so on. Be prepared by arranging something fun with a friend or family member on those particular dates. While you will feel the sting, especially during the first year, time moves on. You might always have the memory, but it will become less painful.

From the Frying Pan into the Fire and Back to Getting a Life

Jilia—51 years old

My story is the classic tale of a woman who got dumped by her husband of thirty-one years when he decided to trade up for a younger version. For two years, I wasted my life being bitter and angry, and I spent my precious time with women in similar situations who loved to eat, drink and have pity parties. We were all middle-age women wallowing in our misery, "looking for love in all the wrong places."

The first year after my divorce, I spent my time going out with a group of friends to bars and bed-hopping. We all smelled of a scent called "desperation and insecurity" that interested only the slimiest of creatures, which only compounded our self-esteem issues. I remember feeling so down that I would go with different men just to prove that I was attractive enough to get them in bed. It became very important to have somebody—anybody—touch me and make me feel alive, even if it only lasted fifteen minutes.

The lowest of lows occurred when a group of my lady friends and I went on a junket to Atlantic City. The memory I have is a night spent at the craps tables with a stranger who kept ordering me drinks and asking me to "blow on his dice." After about an hour of losing money, I wound up in his room in a drunken haze. What I remember was a session of oral sex that left me feeling disgusted and scared of who I was becoming. This was my rock bottom, and it was not pretty. The silver lining was that this drunken incident was the catalyst that spurred me into action to get healthy in my head and my body.

The next day I said good-bye to the women with whom I had arrived and left our soirée early to start building myself a new life and a new attitude. I got home in the evening and took a good hard look at myself. I looked tired, out of shape and old. The alcohol I was consuming was becoming habitual and worrisome. Instead of getting depressed about the image in the mirror, it motivated me to start a contract with myself to get healthy. The main demand I made on myself was to go to Alcoholics Anonymous. I had spent enough time feeling sorry for myself and being cruel to my body. I realized I was only burying myself in a hole I would never climb out of if things didn't start to change immediately and dramatically.

The next positive action was to make a list of things I always wanted to do, big or little, and try something different every month. The first item on the list was yoga. Plagued with back problems for years, I was encouraged by my chiropractor to try a class to help with my chronic pain. I joined my local YMCA and attended my first class, which was the first form of exercise my body had experienced in years.

The instructor walked in, and to my surprise he was a young, beautiful man with the most incredible body. This was a beginner's class involving some basic stretching and moves that I could handle. However, the thing that kept me coming back was not the stretching but the instructor. He was required to invade each student's personal space in order to help them strike the perfect pose or stretch. I could hear his breath and smell his scent as he touched and grabbed places such as my hips, abdominal region, upper chest and shoulders. One day in class he straddled me in an attempt to help me with a stretch where I was arching my back. Oh, baby, touch me, touch me, touch me! Can I have another turn, please? I don't feel so comfortable with this pose. By the end of the class I felt so euphoric from the stretching and the hot human contact, I didn't know if I should grab a towel or a cigarette.

After a few months, I started feeling better, and I was getting very comfortable with the moves in class. The instructor invited me to join his more advanced class. Initially I was unsure if I could handle it, but his encouragement was all I needed to jump to the next level. Of course, more "instructor handling" was required with the more advanced moves; no problem there. I was surprised by how much of a workout this was, and my body was actually starting to change. There was weight loss and toning up. I was starting to look and feel great. The image in the mirror was actually smiling back.

Through this process, I completely ditched the singles scene *and spent my time investigating new hobbies. I had plenty of time because my whole circle of friends seemed to disappear after the divorce, outside of a few true blue girlfriends. I took a class for healthy cooking and also signed up for a ceramics class. The best part of all of my new interests and hobbies was the many different people I met. Suddenly I had an entire new network of men and women in my life who had similar interests and whom I really enjoyed spending time with.*

When I stopped looking for love, it happened. I developed a friendship with a man that lasted a few months before we even considered a romance. The ironic thing is that this man was a bit younger, and the sex was phenomenal. Women really do hit their sexual peak later in life. I was also old enough not to be embarrassed about discussing my likes, dislikes and fantasies. At first I thought my boldness would scare him away, but he told me what a turn-on it was. Who knew? While I have no interest in getting married, it is so freeing just to be with someone who totally likes me.

Ultimately, I had to turn my life around after it had been turned upside down. The rewards were more than I hoped for. The feeling of confidence and respect I have for myself now is something I don't think I ever experienced, even when I was married. When it came down to it I guess it was all about electing to make a positive change and choosing to not be miserable. It could have gone either way, but for me, hitting rock bottom scared me into getting the courage to shake everything up. My life is now full and the relationship with my man only adds to my happiness. I know it sounds like a Hallmark card but it's how I feel. It took going through hell and back, but in the end, I emerged happier on the other side.

Lessons Learned:

- Watch out for the downward spiral of depression because it can swallow you up. Beware of self-medicating by using drugs, alcohol, shopping, food, sex, and so on; addiction is not far behind. Get the help you need, and if you can't afford counseling, find the programs in your city that can help you.

- Sometimes you have to hit rock bottom before you can pick yourself up and start over. Instead of praying for a miracle to get you out of your mess, make the miracle happen by changing your perspective and attitude about your situation. Every day wake up with a positive thought, exercise, breathe and smile. Remember that life is short, and at the end of the day this crapola will be a distant memory that made you wiser and stronger. You have another chance at life so make a choice to create one that is filled with adventure and happiness.

- The bar/singles scene can be depressing. Stop looking for love and start loving yourself and doing things that make you happy and healthy. Get involved in activities and hobbies that interest you—chances are you will meet a network of new friends who will enrich your life.

- If you want to be hot market material, you have to feel and look your best. Confidence and self-esteem are like man magnets, so do the work you need to do to get healthy in your head. Take care of your body. If you don't like looking at yourself naked in the mirror, nobody else will.

Dangers of Immediate Gratification

I loved my interview with Jilia because it really struck a chord with what I watched a lot of my divorced friends go through when I was still safely but miserably married. Once I got divorced, I never expected to pay such a high price emotionally and financially to break the chains of love. I remember wanting to scream out, "Somebody, anybody, please rescue me!"

Beware of the temptation to escape from your stress by chemically altering your body with too much food, drink, sex or drugs. There is nothing wrong with a glass of wine to settle your nerves or a pint of ice cream in front of the TV. Just remember to use moderation, you don't want to turn into a drunken pork chop from overindulging to numb your pain and forget your problems. You will only make the climb back up the mountain more difficult.

Another favorite fix for chicks is having a new romance in their lives. Romeo, Romeo, wherefore art thou Romeo? I have seen it and heard it before; girls on the prowl looking for someone to rescue them from themselves before their divorces are even final.

I have experienced that weak moment, thinking, *If only Prince Charming would rescue me from my emotional and financial turmoil.* I met a friend, who had been happily divorced for the last few years, to spill out my feelings over coffee and biscotti. She reminded me of that saying, "Fool me once, shame on you. Fool me twice, shame on me." She told me that she had done that princess in the dungeon routine and it failed miserably. Her advice was to save myself; nobody else was going to get me out of my own shit without expectations.

Watching the desperate, divorced princess dance play out in life for some friends and acquaintances has given me some good insight. Being needy and emotionally bruised is very unattractive and dangerous. If you get involved with someone when you are running scared, chances are you will go from the frying pan into the fire. I have seen women jump into a relationship as a safety net, only to realize their mistake a few months later. Women I talked to who did this said they rebounded into someone similar to their ex or someone who was a control monster all because they thought it would make them feel safe. They only created more problems for themselves and the experience beat down their self-esteem, which was already gasping for air. The lesson learned: A new relationship with someone is not going to save you; a new relationship with yourself will.

I read and walked for miles at night along the beach, writing bad blank verse and searching endlessly for someone wonderful who would step out of the darkness and change my life. It never crossed my mind that that person could be me.

—Anna Quindlen

Embrace Your Single Status

I'm in the doctor's office filling out forms that require a check in the following category: married__ widowed__ divorced__ or single__ . Hmmm, I'm in a new people category. I am divorced and suddenly single, and I have to report it to a complete stranger. I'd been checking the married space so long, it was the first time I really considered the intrusiveness of the question. I felt unsettled and ostracized that I was now being asked to check off into the divorced and single category.

After a few slow deep breaths I started to wonder why I had such a negative reaction to checking off divorced and single to the world. After all, almost half the people in America now fall in my category; I'm actually in good company. What about those people who are checking off "married" and wishing they were in my category? I decided to make the most of my new status in society, but it did take some getting used to. The good news was that I spent a lot of time alone in my marriage so I had a good head start, but I still felt a bit like a displaced person—I had to find myself.

What I learned is that finding yourself is a process and it takes time. Part of the journey is to appreciate your own company as you learn to venture into the world and enjoy life as a single person. When you do the work of emotional healing, you start to feel good about who you are. You want to come out from the rock you've been hiding under and enjoy the social life you remember being part of when you were married, but now you are suddenly alone. The challenge is to get off the couch and do things you enjoy even if it's on your own. At first going to a movie or dinner alone can be awkward, but you get to pick what you want to do without dealing with somebody else. Once you do it you feel liberated and it will be more comfortable to do it again.

I love tennis and there was a charity event in my town I had always gone to as a married person. I thought I could never go on my own. It was my weekend without my children, and I was feeling incredibly alone and sorry for myself. I tried to make plans, but all my friends were busy with their lives and families. Once again I resigned myself to Ben and Jerry's ice cream on the couch with my dog and Lifetime television. As I sat there staring out at the beautiful day, I had finally had enough. I got my ass out of the house and drove myself to the tennis match. I bought my ticket, found my seat and had a great time. I introduced myself to the people sitting next to me, and they invited me to have lunch with them, and we all enjoyed the day. I was so happy that I didn't waste my free day in the house, and it gave me the courage to go on more adventures on my own.

Most of us will not remain single forever. We may choose to marry again or just share time with others as they come in and out of our lives. Being single is actually a great time to get in touch with who you are and focus on what you want. After divorce, this time is very important for your recovery and ability to have healthier relationships in the future. Being single is not a hardship, for most of us it's a temporary time in our lives we should embrace and enjoy before we choose otherwise.

Chapter 6

The Children

*There is always a moment in childhood
when the door opens and lets the future in.*

—Graham Greene

There is no getting around it; divorce is difficult for children. As parents we feel tremendous guilt as we share their heartache. On the flip side, children suffer in homes with the tension of unhappily married parents. The topic of staying together for the sake of the children is very controversial. I had many uncomfortable conversations with my predivorce friends, who were miserable in their own marriages. We were practically screaming at each other as some justified their married existence for the sake of the children, while others considered divorce in order to provide a healthier environment for their children and a chance for their own happiness. Judgment and fear were being thrown around the room, fueled by negative studies and stigmas concerning children and divorce.

The reality is that our fancy statistics and clinical studies will never be able to make a final judgment. We can never look at a child and compare whether their childhood would be healthier and happier with parents who stay together in miserable matrimony versus the same child who grows up with divorce. We don't live in parallel worlds, and to compare both scenarios is impossible. The answer will always be hypothetical at best.

As parents, we have an opportunity and responsibility to help our children as their family configuration changes and they learn to adapt to their new circumstances. We can minimize the negative effects if we focus on putting our children first. This can be accomplished by being a strong adult figure in the house, maintaining a civil relationship with our former spouse and making every effort to keep children out of the middle.

Taming the Guilt Monster

If you are the one who left a bad marriage, remember this:

- Children are more capable of adapting to change than adults.
- Studies are now showing that children living in low-conflict, divorced families grow up with fewer problems than children living in high-conflict families that stay together.

Divorce does not have to adversely affect children to the extent society tells us it will. Children will do as well as their parents do as they lead the way into a new life. We always hear about emotional growth resulting from bad things that happen and are out of our control. Divorce is no different. As parents we need to stop focusing on our guilt and put our energy into having a positive attitude. When we feel better about our situations, we will be better prepared to guide our children as they journey into their new life feeling safe, secure and loved.

With strong parental figures, a child can walk away from divorce with strength, understanding and a more realistic view of the world. In the interviews that I did with older children and young adults of divorced families, they said they learned and gained the following, which has helped them in their lives:

- They learned at an early age that life is not always fair. This idea helped them to deal with life's disappointments and to have a greater appreciation for good times. They became stronger and more adaptable to the many changes and twists they had to deal with in life.
- Their experience took them on a completely different path in life where they met new people and had different experiences. They became more realistic about the complexity of relationships as they learned from their parents' experience. Some kids experienced blended families, which many said was difficult at times, but it was also great to have more people in their lives.
- Surprisingly, on some levels they enjoyed the new family configuration, which allowed more quality time alone with each parent. They also grew closer to their siblings because they could talk to each other with real understanding.
- Children growing up in divorce follow several stages that move from fear, to anger, to acceptance and, most important, to adaptation. Somebody once told me that divorce with children is like throwing a stone into a perfectly calm lake. The ripple moves through the entire body of water and everything is affected. The aftermath can be rough until the waters calm down again.

Lauren—29 years old

My parents divorced when I was ten and it rocked my world. The unconditional love and patience they both gave me was what got me through the difficult transition. I felt that they were always a team when it came to me, whether I liked it or not. I remember both houses having the same rules, and when I tried to play one parent against the other I always lost.

The most difficult thing for me was not having a sibling to share my feelings and commiserate with. I told my mother how I felt so all alone and different from everyone else who lived in one house, not two. My mom found a program through the school system where a guidance counselor provided group therapy for kids of divorce. This was very helpful for me because I no longer felt alienated. There were other kids there with the same set of circumstances more or less. It was powerful to know that I was not alone, and I developed friendships that I still treasure today.

Both of my parents remarried a few years later, and that was another difficult transition. My unrealistic dream of them getting back together was completely destroyed as these new people came into their lives. I was nasty and out of control, my life was interrupted again and I was forced to deal with new people and circumstances. Once the dust settled and I accepted yet another change, these new people were actually wonderful additions to my life.

The one thing that sticks out in my head is that both new spouses to my parents never tried to take away from either of my parents. They were very respectful of our relationship and never had a bad word or expressed bad feelings in front of me. I have wonderful memories and pictures of my entire family and all of the extensions that come with it. We were small, nuclear and miserable. Now we are blended, happy and expansive.

Watching my parents take a chance to love again and create new families was difficult at the time. As I grew up, I realized that they showed me by example that love, mutual understanding and respect are basic things one should expect in relationships. What I lived through and learned help me to make better choices in my life. I found a great partner in marriage, and that makes me happy. I hope I can give my children everything my parents gave me.

Lessons Learned

- Each situation is different and, sometimes, divorcing may be the least damaging to a child. Let's face it, it's inevitable that we will screw up our children to some degree no matter what we do or don't do. It's called being human, so stop dwelling on the guilt and start looking for ways to help your children learn to roll with the punches.

It is not a parent's job to protect their kids from life but to prepare them for it.

—Blake Segal

Getting a Parental Grip

Raising kids is part joy—and part guerrilla warfare.

—Ed Asner

The biggest challenge is to be your children's rock during a time when you feel like you are about to lose your mind. During the transition, your kids are dealing with their own issues and emotions. There is definitely pain and loss for children; they will need time to grieve and experience their pain before moving on. As their parent, you need to give your children time and space to do this, which will require much of your patience and energy. You have to be in a good place yourself to do this and find the strength to help them get through this difficult time.

It can be a recipe for disaster as they test you and watch to see how you are going to stand up to them and the new reality you all face. What they need from you right now is for you to be a strong parent. Don't use your children as your emotional support—they are not miniature adults. The last thing you want to do is switch roles where they feel this incredible burden of making sure you are all right. It scares them, and it's just not their job. It's an easy trap to fall into so remember to let them be children and keep them out of the adult world of problems. Find the appropriate support system through friends, family and organizations to help get you through this time. Do what you need to get yourself in a good place so you can regain your strength. You can't give to your children what you don't have yourself.

It will be very important for your children to express their feelings. Sharing your own feelings (with much editing) will encourage them to share as well. Don't be afraid to be honest and let them hear that you are sad about the family breaking up. Follow up with some positive thoughts and ideas of how the situation will get better. Some children will require counseling to help them through the adjustment period. It's important that they express their feelings and deal with their emotions; otherwise, it just comes back to haunt them and you. For those of you with an only child, keep in mind that they have no sibling to commiserate with. Group counseling with children in similar circumstances can be very helpful so they know they are not alone.

The Right Words, the Right Time, the Right Place

Many parents put themselves under a lot of pressure when they think about the talk they need to have with their children about the upcoming separation. They get freaked out that if they say the wrong words, their children will be set on the path to impending doom and misery. It simply requires some common sense and plenty of love.

The most important thing you can do is to break the news with your spouse as a family without assigning blame. Come from the heart with honesty and assure them that their relationship with both parents will continue (if possible). Pick an appropriate time and place they feel safe so there will be plenty of time to answer their questions. Ask them about their fears and concerns and address them the best you can with the constant reassurance you will always love them and that the divorce was not their fault. Don't fall into the trap of giving them false hope you might get back together again just to make them feel better.

Divorce is confusing for children, so don't overload them with too much information. Give them basic information so they understand you will continue to take care of them and love them the same way. Remember, "The Talk" will never go exactly how you planned, and your children's reactions will be painful to see. Allow plenty of time for hugs and kisses and explain again that it was an adult decision that had nothing to do with them.

Information you give your children should always be age appropriate. As the years pass and they grow up, they might ask for more specific details of your breakup. This can be difficult, but you want to remain honest as you try not to bad-mouth their other parent. Kids are very smart. Give them the basics without focusing on the negative, and they will fill in the holes for themselves. Always keep the lines of communication open. Leaving children in the dark can be harmful because their imaginations will likely make up realities that are much worse than what really happened. This can leave children angry and confused which can affect their future relationships and how they see their world.

Books are a great tool to use when talking about divorce. Always read each book from beginning to end to make sure you are comfortable with the information. Here are some suggestions:

Three to seven years old: *It's Not Your Fault, KoKo Bear*
By Vicky Lansky, 1998, Book Peddlers

School-age children: *Dinosaurs Divorce: A Guide for Changing Families*
By Laurene Drasney Brown and Marc Brown, 1986
Little, Brown and Company

Older school-age children: *How Do I Feel About: My Parents' Divorce*
By Julia Cole, 1997, Copper Beech Books

Preteen: *Pre-Teen Pressures: Divorce*
By Debra Goldentyer, 1998, Steck Vaughn

There is a great catalog called *Child's Work, Child's Play* that provides great tools such as books and board games to help your children adapt to the change. Showing them that there are other children in similar situations will keep them from feeling alienated.

It's important to paint a picture for children of how their immediate future will look. Explain their new living arrangements, how much time they will be spending with each parent, and what holidays and vacations will look like. Let them have access to your soon-to-be ex's extended family. The more people in a child's life who support and love them, the better off they will be. Don't ever ask a child to choose who they want to live with; it's not fair to put them in that position. Prepare them with books and games before the actual separation and try to spend some extra time together. Continue to do the family rituals; make having fun a priority with your kids. Do the best you can to prepare your children for the upcoming changes and don't forget to check yourself—separating for the first child visitation will be very difficult on all of you.

Child Alert

As mentioned, the most difficult part of divorce and separation is watching your children struggle with the emotional process that is ongoing and ever-changing. On some level, it will never be okay for them, even when things seem to be running smoothly. They will always dream that their parents will get back together. The idea of their parent meeting someone new is too much for them to handle in the beginning.

In the beginning of the divorce and separation, kids are feeling anxious and overwhelmed. To help them through their process, you need to have an idea of what goes on in their heads and some of the issues they struggle with. When I interviewed children, I was surprised at how in touch they were with their feelings and what was going on.

The most difficult thing for kids is not seeing both parents every day. They also have a lot of frustration with the constant shuffling back and forth to both houses with all of their stuff they can't seem to keep track of. Their friends never seem to know where to find them and which phone number to reach them at. They complain about having more responsibilities around the house and having less money as they watch both parents struggle to get by. They particularly resent being put in the middle of their parents' issues and listening to them argue, especially over money.

I was also surprised to learn how much guilt and anger they felt. Kids feel bad about leaving a parent at home alone to go out with their friends or visit their other parent, especially during the holidays. Many kids don't like watching their parents go out on dates. One boy said he gets very angry at his parents for being selfish and disrupting his life and then feels guilty about having those feelings. It makes him feel confused, and sometimes he takes his crazy feelings out on his parents, siblings and friends.

My interviews with other children and watching my own children struggle with similar issues is heartbreaking. It certainly drives home the fact that divorce is not just about our struggles adjusting to a new life but theirs as well. It's not so much the divorce but the afterlife and how both parents behave as the situation settles down and the family takes on a new configuration.

It's important for your children to see you acting civil and, if possible, friendly toward one another. Be aware that you walk a fine line as they watch and listen to your every move. While you don't want them to see you fighting, you also don't want to give them false hope that the two of you might get back together. If you are going to spend time together as a family, you must set boundaries with your ex, as well as your children, You must reinforce and communicate that your together time is for special times and it does not mean you will be getting back together.

My ex and I both have significant others in our lives who the children enjoy being with. However, this will never change their dream, even if they know how unrealistic it is, that we might get back together again. I know a teenage girl whose parents have been divorced for seven years. They are both seriously involved with other people. Yet on her dressing table in her room still stands a beautiful heart frame with a picture of her mother and father hugging.

One of the most difficult scenarios for children is when parents break up, only to get back together for a short time and then break up all over again. While there is nothing wrong with trying to salvage a relationship, it's important for you to keep in mind how the children will be affected when they see mommy and daddy sleeping in the same bed.

Many couples have a transitional time together before the actual end where they still see each other and sometimes sleep together. If this is something you are doing knowing that you will never get back together again, spare the children from seeing you together. It's too confusing and painful to see their parents ping-pong back and forth. The pain they experience is bad enough the first time they hear their parents are splitting up; don't magnify their pain by making them experience it all over again.

Child Custody and Visitation Schedules

This can be a very sticky and difficult part of the divorce process. It's especially unfair to children because they are not the ones getting divorced yet they suffer the majority of the consequences. Children get damaged by divorce the most when parents battle over custody arrangements. Unless a parent is a threat or unfit, do your best to work out a schedule without dragging it into court and save your family from the emotional and financial hardship!

However, there are instances where intervention by the courts can be a blessing if there is a parent who is a danger or unfit to be a caregiver. If you have any concerns about their dad being a fit parent, you owe it to your children to fight for custody. The worst-case scenario, which rarely happens, is to have children testify in court. Although unpleasant, their testimony might be the key that keeps them away from a potentially dangerous parent. Sometimes, a stranger in a courtroom can decide what is best for children and protect them from being put in harm's way. If money is a problem, there are services and legal aid you can find in your community at minimal or no cost. If all else fails, you can represent your children by alerting a judge in the courtroom about your concerns.

Unfortunately, the majority of custody battles are fueled by anger and revenge, using children as ammunition. Parents give up complete control to someone they don't know to decide what is best for their family just to get back at their spouse. Using the court for these reasons only hurts the children and costs a fortune. Most judges hate having to make these difficult choices, but they do. Think about that for a minute, a total stranger is determining what is best for your child. Ask yourself if what you are fighting for is worth an end result that is unpredictable and totally out of your control.

Regardless of your reasons, if you do go to battle over your children, there are new laws concerning child support and custody that might surprise you. First of all, the courts very rarely have children testify in an open court. They avoid putting them in stressful situations and do so only on special request. Instead a new system is now in place that is becoming more common in many states. The court will assign a child evaluator to the family. The cost is about $500 for each parent, and it's a process that can take up to three months. This person conducts interviews and home visits to make an objective opinion as to what is best for the children. A judge may or may not agree with the opinion. This system is intrusive but helps create a better picture of how the children relate to each parent and keeps them out of a court room. The goal is to make an educated decision that will hopefully benefit the children.

There also is a new trend concerning child visitation and support.

Child visitation guidelines are the minimum the courts would like to see the noncustodial parent exercise. If the father requests more than the minimum schedule, and the court believes the father is a capable parent, they will likely grant visitation that is a 50/50 split. With that comes a new law many states now have that will decrease child support payments depending on what the split is.

Traditionally, the schedule determines the amount of child support based solely on the father's salary. Depending on your state, if the father gets more than minimum time by 30 percent or more, the charts are adjusted for a reduction of payment based on that percentage. This is where you have to hope the dad is asking for more time because of his love for his kids, not the money. Courts will rarely give custody to the father or make him the primary caregiver unless there is good reason and proof that the mother is unfit as a parent.

Most states follow a traditional schedule the court system created with the guidance of child psychologists. A primary caregiver is designated, and the other parent, usually the father, has visitation every other weekend—Thursday after school with drop-off at school Monday morning. On his off weekend, the children get picked up after school on Thursday and dropped off at school Friday morning. Children and parents do best when there is flexibility and the ability to reach their parent by phone anytime.

Initially, not having your children by your side every day can make you feel fearful and sick to your stomach. The most difficult part is the total loss of control you have over your children, especially when they are young. I was very lucky because my ex turned out to be one of those dads who rose to the occasion after the divorce. When my children are with him, I know they are in great hands and I can relax. It wasn't easy to let go in the beginning, and to this day I still struggle sometimes. Eventually, it all works out; especially when I remember to roll with situations and circumstances as they come up.

For example, as I sit here and write these words, my ex is on vacation with my children and his girlfriend in Colorado. There is a flu epidemic and the terror alert has just been raised to orange. My youngest has been sick with a fever and sounds like he is miserable.

Does this make me happy? No. Do I have control? No. Do I feel like I'm going to go out of my mind, YES!! I have learned over time that I have no other choice but to control my level of anxiety and feel confident they will arrive home safe and happy.

Visitation Schedules in the Real World

The best-case scenario is two parents who want to be active co-parents in their children's lives and can peacefully come to terms on visitation without court intervention. In our case, the court-ordered visitation turned out to be a schedule on paper that would be enforced only if we couldn't come to terms with each other. To this day we don't follow it, but we have our own consistent schedule to keep everyone's life predictable. We worked out what's best for the children so they are not constantly bounced from house to house. We also make sure we give each other the opportunity to take the kids rather than leave them with a babysitter. The kids' extracurricular activities provide more time to see them on our off days. During the holidays we alternate, but sometimes we split the day up. This way the children enjoy two parties and get to see family on both sides, so nobody feels like they missed out.

Some families can actually share the holidays together with all of the extensions that come along, including new girlfriends, wives, boyfriends and husbands. Personally, I'm not there and don't think I ever will be. I feel more comfortable having boundaries in place but feel quite comfortable sharing important events like graduations, weddings, Sweet Sixteens, and so on. Everyone will have their own comfort level for what works for them and feelings should be respected.

Many times visitation simply becomes some version of the court order that changes over time as new situations present themselves. Here are some creative examples of how cooperative parents worked out visitation for their families:

- Some families don't like the constant bouncing back and forth every few days. They opt for more consistent time with children by going one or two weeks at a time. This works when the off parent has access to children for carpooling, dinner, dessert and the like.

The off parent must make a conscious effort to stay involved in the children's lives during their off time to stay connected. Most children prefer this arrangement because it keeps their stuff and homework in one place and their friends know where they are.

- Some parents experiment with unconventional living arrangements. For financial reasons, some parents choose to share the marital home. This requires the parents to have an unusual amount of respect and ability to get along to even consider such a scenario. Some parents share the same living quarters in different parts of the house. This is usually very time limited until one parent can get their feet on the ground and move on. Most families don't do well in this scenario for the long term.

- An unusual scenario is when the children stay in the marital home and the parents visit the children. This requires a second residence, which is usually an apartment where the off parent lives until it's his or her time for visitation. Essentially, the parents share the apartment, and they are the ones burdened with the back and forth, while the children enjoy one residence. Again, a very unique and unusual situation. This will likely work well in the beginning to transition the children, but will be time limited as each parent moves on with their lives or just gets fed up.

- Unfortunately sometimes one parent moves to another state for work or personal reasons. Children can do well if the off parent communicates frequently by phone and e-mail. This leaves visitation during holidays and summer vacations. This becomes a challenge for the primary caregiver who will feel they get all work and no play time with their kids. Some families actually take some family vacations together. The awkwardness of separate rooms, being together and food bills overrides an opportunity for both parents to enjoy their kids when school is out. There are some interesting models out there like Demi Moore and Bruce Willis. Their kids obviously come first, and the parents have grown to have a unique relationship that seems to work for their adapted family. Each person must decide what works for them.

Ultimately, you have to do what's best for the kids and comfortable for you as far as spending time together. As mentioned earlier, some families take vacations together and stay in separate rooms soon after the divorce to help ease the transition. Some parents have keys to the other's home in case a child forgets something and has to get in while the other is out of town or at work. Some co-parents can only manage ice cream after soccer games together.

In the end, nothing is more important than both parents' presence to help celebrate a child's big and little accomplishments in an atmosphere free of conflict. The most important togetherness coparents can display for children is to let them see parents who are on the same page with rules and expectations.

It's important to mention the manipulation and guilt that our sweet little children will hurl at us. While it's normal behavior and happens in the nuclear family, it seems compounded with interest in the divorced situation. The one thing you have to prepare and brace yourself for is the conversations about how much they hate living in two houses. This comes with a painful side of tears and begging to make it better and go back to the way it was. This, of course, is very individual and age dependent, but there will be some degree of mutiny, either direct or indirect. Let them know that, while there are many things you would like to do for them and help them with, this one is not possible and the situation is not changing. Let them know you hear them, tell them you understand how hard the situation is and that it's hard for you also. Children feel better if they simply know you understand what they are feeling.

Divorce is difficult for children. Suddenly, sometimes without warning, their lives are turned completely upside down. They can't see both parents every day and they are shuttled from house to house every few days. While they are very adaptive, it's a challenging situation so allow them the time and space to vent and act out a bit. It's painful and gives you an incredible feeling of helplessness. The best way you can help is to listen and let them know you understand how they feel, but don't give them false hope.

Elizabeth—41 years old

I think I participate in one of the most unique child custody arrangements. I have a fourteen-year-old stepdaughter I started raising when she was only four years old. I married her dad when I was in my late twenties, and to this day I wonder if I fell in love with the man or his sweet little girl. After the first few dates I learned that his ex-wife left their daughter when she was only two years old. The mom has very little contact with her and wants no responsibility as a parent. The only real mother she knows is me and I have been exactly that, her mom. I couldn't love this girl any more if she were my own flesh and blood.

A few years into our marriage, her dad and I started having problems. Our relationship slowly unraveled and I found myself on the way to being separated. Leaving him was not going to be a problem—the fear was losing her. Luckily my ex was lost without my help and support as his daughter's mother. When we started negotiating the separation, he welcomed my proposed arrangement for visitation. We agreed that I would move out of the house and into an apartment of my own. I would have visitation with my daughter every weekend and have some open time for dinner during the week if possible.

Telling Sarah was something that kept me up at night, but her reaction was quite surprising. Her first question was if I was going to still be her mom as tears streaked down her cheeks. We assured her that nothing was going to stop me from being with her, and when she heard our schedule she settled down a bit. A few seconds later she looked panicked again and asked if she was still going to see my side of the family (cousins, grandparents, etc.). We said, of course, they would not stop being her family. She nodded her head and said, "Yeah, I'm not the one getting the divorce, you are."

The rest was easy as she took over the conversation. She told us she wasn't surprised, she knew we weren't happy and that it was only a matter of when we would break up. Like a mature little lady, she looked at us puffy and sad with a little pout. She told us she would eventually be all right as long as both of us would continue to be her parents and she could still see my family.

The transition was harder than I thought for all of us, but in time things settled down and our routine became familiar and comfortable. I am a big part of her life, we talk every day and see each other often. During our weekend visits, there is always one day we have a family get-together at my parents' house for dinner. For special holidays, I have been invited over to my husband's parents' house to help celebrate with our daughter. His family is very good to me even though the situation can be awkward at times.

I guess I don't think about how unconventional our situation is until I start talking to some friends about my life. My soon-to-be ex switched jobs and has been doing a lot of traveling. There have been times during the week that he needs coverage for Sarah and staying at my apartment was just too far from her school. He suggested we stay in his house, our old house, the one that has only two bedrooms. The proposition was uncomfortable, but there was really no other choice.

The first night was a game of musical beds. First I started off on the couch, with Sarah trying to sleep in her twin bed as she kept calling out to me wondering if I was comfortable. The couch was not comfortable, so I jumped into bed with her. That lasted maybe five minutes after we lay there like packed sardines. She looked at me and we both laughed as we considered her dad's big, king size bed just waiting for us in the other room. After two seconds of consideration, our exhaustion took over, and within five minutes we were sleeping soundly in a big comfy bed.

This has been going on for the last year. Most of the time, I don't think about it because it's all a bit too strange and in the "how did this become my life" category. The good news is that Sarah has a great relationship with both of us and has adjusted better than we thought. While my weekends get cramped a bit for my own social life, I see openings coming up now that she is older and she has slumber parties and movie nights out with her friends.

Sarah and I have an incredible mother/daughter bond that will never be broken. I find it hard to break away from my husband not because I think our marriage can work but because of our child-care routine. There is so much communication needed between us to make things work for Sarah, it's hard to cut the cord. Now that she is getting older, I can see that things will take their course and more space will set us on separate paths.

Our little girl has faced many challenges starting at a young age, but she is growing into a fine young lady who is happy and ready to take on life. The situations I have been in with my soon-to-be ex have been a bit over the top at times. However, for the sake of Sarah, I wouldn't have changed a thing. Through this process, there have been many times I felt like screaming, even running. What stopped me was thinking about my daughter's smile and a saying we always had in my house when I was growing up as a kid: "Sometimes you just have to SUCK IT UP."

Lessons Learned

- The suck-it-up motto: During moments when a situation makes you want to scream profanities, run away or start hurling the nearest heavy object, you simply take a deep breath, smile and act like the adult you are because you have no choice.
- When you are faced with doing something that might make you uncomfortable but will benefit your children, do it. Remember they didn't get divorced, you did.

The Single Parent's Learning Curve

Learning to be a single parent is an adjustment and process that takes time. There are unique circumstances that take some getting used to as you move into your new role with your ex and your children. It's a challenge that comes with good things, not such great things and the unexpected. Practical experience will be your best teacher.

Absentee Dad

Some of you will be completely on your own if your ex disappears and turns out to be an absentee father. This situation will be more challenging for you and your children if you face the entire emotional and financial burden of raising your children on your own. Out of necessity, you will have to create a support system through your family and friends to help you manage all of your responsibilities. If you are new to the area, you can find support in your community through religious organizations and groups for single parents. This will help you create a whole network of friends for yourself and your children because you really can't do it all on your own.

You will have to be extra vigilant to keep your children out of the world of adult problems so they can enjoy their childhood. As I mentioned earlier, your kids are not mini-adults for you to talk about your problems with. When you feel overwhelmed, find an adult you can talk to, and don't be afraid to ask for help because you will need it. Having somebody to count on for babysitting or that middle of the night run to the emergency room with a sick child is a necessity when you are a single parent.

Many women who have traveled this road said that while it was difficult, there were also some positives that came along with all the responsibility. For instance, they enjoyed having the freedom to make all of the decisions regarding their children. Also, many moms said they enjoyed a much tighter bond with their kids as they faced the world together and everyone in the family really counted on each other. While their kids had more responsibilities at home, they were always acknowledged for their efforts and grew up into self-sufficient adults.

All of the women I talked to said ideally it would have been nice for the children to have their dad in their lives and to share the responsibilities. Some women were relieved to be alone because their exes would have caused harm to their children. Others simply had no choice because their ex just disappeared. Regardless of the situation, many women learned to stand strong and managed to raise healthy, happy kids on their own with the help and support from family and friends.

Smart Choices, Unexpected Rewards

My attorney told me about his experience with men, their children and divorce. He said men will either drift away from their kids' lives or become father of the year. If your ex is a good father and wants to be in the children's lives, consider yourself lucky and do everything to encourage their relationship. It is in the best interest of the children for their father to be a big part of their lives as long as it's not a harmful relationship.

Learning to compartmentalize your anger and frustration with your children's father is one of the smartest things you can do; it's all about forgiveness and letting go of the past. The peace that comes from doing this will trickle down to your children as they learn and benefit from a parent who is not filled with anger and moves on with their new life.

Kids need both of their parents in their lives as much as possible. Lashing out, being nasty and asking your children to choose sides will make it more difficult for their dad to remain a constant in their lives and share half of the responsibility with you as a co-parent. Your children are watching your every move and listening to your every word. Don't bite your nose off to spite your face because in the end you and your children will suffer. Keep in mind that if you don't do right by your kids, it will come back to haunt you when they get older and resent you for chasing their dad away.

Transitioning from Spouse to Co-parent

The best-case scenario is having a good dad who wants to continue in his role after the divorce. This is great news for you because you have a partner who is willing to share the responsibilities of raising your children. The kids benefit by having him in their lives in more of a one-on-one relationship because, during his visitation time, it's all up to him. This gives fathers a real opportunity to connect and spend quality time with their kids.

The transition from spouse to co-parent, in the beginning especially, can be quite challenging. The first step starts with changing your expectations of one another. I remember a song that said old lovers can be good friends. I believe it, but I didn't realize it takes time and respecting each other's need for space. I struggled with this in the beginning because I expected my ex to be my friend too soon.

He moved out of the house a few weeks before September 11th. He was one of my first calls when the news hit and we raced to each child's school to pick them up. Once we had them in my house happily munching on snacks and watching a video, I desperately wanted him to sit down with me and commiserate about the terrorist attack. His response was to walk out of the house after kissing the kids good-bye.

I was left in a frightened heap. I felt incredibly lost, alone and angry. He was great with the kids, but suddenly I was treated like a stranger because it was no longer his job to comfort me and assure me of our kids' future. It hit me hard that night as I lay in bed alone watching replay after replay of the planes crashing into the Twin Towers. I had a great support system but still had to deal with the transition of being alone without an adult's immediate presence in the bed next to me.

At the time, I didn't consider that he needed to draw a line in the sand in order to deal with the breakup. His healing process required him to stay away from me as much as possible in the beginning until his new life became a bit settled. Looking back, I certainly didn't help matters by asking him to help me with things around a house that was now mine, not his. At the time I couldn't understand what the big deal was for him to get on a ladder and change a lightbulb. The problem was that it was all about me and what I was going through. I was too self-absorbed to consider his experience and what he had to deal with.

My understanding came after a big fight when he told me how angry he was that he had to move out of the house into an apartment. He was the one who was uprooted from his home and children, not me. No, it was not okay for me to call him for small talk or ask him to fix the TV. He went on for a few more minutes and I felt like a shit. I was so insensitive; it was like pouring salt on his wounds. From that speech on, I realized that I could no longer rely on him for myself, only with the children, and I was grateful for that. Over time, our new relationship has had its share of growing pains. It seems to be an ongoing process of adapting to life as our children get older and things change as new people come into our lives. There's never a dull moment, but our relationship has gotten easier as there are clearer boundaries of what we can expect from each other.

Parental Checkpoints

It's easy to get self-absorbed during the process of divorce. It's so important to be there for your children. Every day I would remind myself to ask my children how they were doing. Even though I was mentally and physically exhausted, I tried to give them some quality time. Something as simple as snuggling next to them while they watched TV was like a magical pick-me-up for all of us.

Make it a habit to talk to your children and ask them how they feel about different situations and issues as they come up. The more they are comfortable talking to you, the more likely they will come to you with their problems. If you feel like your children need extra help, get them counseling. Tell them every day how much you love them and give them at least one specific compliment every day.

Be careful not to spoil out of feelings of guilt. Discipline your children when appropriate. Children need rules, and they want to see that you are in charge and acting out your role as parent. Part of your role as a strong parent requires you to be a mature adult. Never argue with your ex in front of the kids. Your kids can feel any anger or bad feelings you have toward one another, so watch it. Try to establish a civil if not friendly relationship with your ex as a co-parent.

> *We are divorced, we are friends,*
> *we are good parents.*
>
> —Sarah Ferguson

My parental wake-up call came in the middle of battling my ex during our divorce when I picked up my children after they had spent a weekend with their dad. There was a lot of tension between us, and while we rarely fought in front of the kids there was definitely a sharp coldness in the air. At the next weekend drop off, things between us had settled down and I was feeling good, the air between us was a bit lighter. As I drove away, my four-year-old looked at me and said, "Mommy, I'm proud of you for being so nice to Daddy today."

I almost started to cry because I realized how much my little children understood and watched as their parents interacted. I realized that children are like little creatures with instinctual senses; they can smell the anger on you no matter how hard you try to cover it up. That day I made myself a promise to do my best to separate my anger from the business of divorce and do my best to let go and get along with my ex. If my ex and I raise our voices or have a problem with each other, my kids immediately jump all over it and ask us to stop. It's a great way to diffuse our hostility when we take our children's advice to just get along, which is what we have always taught them.

While we are not perfect, we are civil and somewhat friendly for the sake of the kids. We both realized the potential damage of anger or hate between us was just too great. We also realized that our children are attached to us by the hip for the rest of our lives and we needed to find a better way to relate to each other. While it's not always easy and there are many hurdles to overcome, we are doing a great job because I think we both learned to pick our battles and let things go.

> *Your children will see what you're all about*
> *by what you live rather than what you say.*
>
> —Dr. Wayne Dyer

The ideal transition is easier if there is a cooperative former spouse. However, we have no guarantee or control over someone else's behavior now or in the future. The only things we will ever have control over are our choices and actions.

Co-parent Etiquette

Emily Post should have a chapter on divorce and how to deal with your ex and the "significant other" factor. Soon after the separation or divorce, you could find yourself in unfamiliar and very uncomfortable waters. There are many potential situations that can be confusing for children and difficult for both parents to deal with.

The next few pages will prepare you for what to expect and how to keep your cool in unusual and challenging situations. The main thing is to use common sense, diplomacy, put your children first and always try to put yourself in the other parent's shoes. Consider how a potential scenario might make you feel before doing something that might cause damage.

R-e-s-p-e-c-t

I don't care what your issues were when you were married. The relationship has changed, and your roles and expectations of each other are completely different. As the married partnership falls apart, a new partnership must be formed as co-parents. In the beginning of the transition, how you treat each other will be the foundation of how your newly configured family will function. Trying to get it right from the beginning will only benefit you and your children.

If you want respect, you have to give it and be worthy of respect yourself. This, of course, guarantees nothing because you have no control over how the other person will respond. The only control you do have is over your actions. When conflicts arise with your co-parent—and they will—try to be respectful. To start, I always try to refer to the children as "our children," not "my children." I think that's just a matter of respect, and his ears will most likely be more open to what I have to say. While it's not a marriage anymore, it's still a relationship you have to work on to keep the harmony, so choose your battles wisely. Otherwise, it's very easy to fight about everything, and then you are living in the same relationship you got away from.

I know one woman who would practice on a tape recorder before discussing big issues with her co-parent. It can avoid communication remorse when you play back words and hear a tone you can't believe came out of your mouth. Communication will not always be easy, but you will make the extra effort when you remember that your children are watching and listening closely to your interaction with their dad. Let them see you do the right thing regardless of the situation. You will be role-modeling how to treat others in difficult situations.

Some of you might find divorce with children requires more work than your marriage. To review, here are the top five rules we have already touched upon to create and maintain a low-conflict, respectful co-parent relationship.

1. If your ex is in your children's lives, don't allow them to call your significant other Dad, Daddy, Father or anything close. Hopefully you will get the same treatment in return.

2. Never talk badly about their father, period. If children ask questions, do your best to give honest answers without judgment while being age appropriate.
3. Always give your ex the first right of refusal of doing something special with your children before asking a significant other to do it. For example, taking your teenage daughter for her driver's test.
4. If possible, try to celebrate birthdays, graduations and special events together. Take into consideration each other's comfort issues and pick a place that will eliminate stress so you can enjoy your children and give them a sense of family.
5. Learn to pick your battles with your ex when it comes to the children. Get a feeling for what is worth discussing and what you actually have no control over.

Communication

If you are lucky enough to have an ex-spouse who is a great parent and plays an active role in your children's lives, communication and coordination are key. There will be countless drop-offs, pickups, sporting events, dance recitals, doctor's appointments and play dates. It will become necessary to work as a team, especially as you transition them and their "stuff" from one house to the other. Don't be surprised if you actually talk more now than when you were married.

Out of necessity you have to get organized. Get a good calendar book to schedule visitation, holidays, special events and vacations with your co-parent. There is a lot of give and take when it comes to sharing the kids and taking some time off for your own vacations. You want to be flexible but still stay on a predictable schedule for everyone's sanity.

While you'll have the majority of responsibility during your "on parent time," at times a joint effort will be necessary. It's almost impossible to work with a schedule of who is doing what without a calendar. Inevitably, there will be the occasional "I thought you were picking up John" panic moment. During special occasions or when you are squeezed for time, it's helpful to do a dry run the night before with your ex to avoid the following chaotic scenario.

My ex was taking the kids on vacation for the first time without me. He was meeting me to pick up the kids right after he left work. The night before, we spoke briefly about where we would meet for pickup. Plans changed several times during the conversation, but I was clear on what I was doing and what he was doing. The problem was that my ex heard a different game plan than I proposed.

Time was short for them to make their flight. When my ex pulled up and he saw me looking for my youngest child in the backseat, he freaked and yelled, "I thought you were picking up the kids!" It was a frantic race as we figured out a new game plan, and I realized just how close he was cutting his time.

I rushed to the preschool and met him near to the highway looking and feeling like a "frazzled Frida." I pulled up, pleased that I arrived sooner than anticipated, only to be met by his girlfriend in the passenger seat smiling at me like a Cheshire cat. I thought he would be relieved to see us, but the anger was still there because he realized the bag I packed for my sons did not have some things they needed for the trip. The most important was my oldest son's Game Boy, which would help keep everyone's sanity during the five-hour plane ride. At that moment, I started to wonder how his girlfriend would entertain my children on their long journey.

My ex put the blame all on me for not knowing exactly what he would need for the trip. I explained that I was not a mind reader and that we needed more communication to avoid another stressful scenario in the future. In the end it was a bit of a fiasco but he apologized and we learned our lesson. Now, the night before a big event we do a dry run of what is needed and who is doing what. The one thing we are more careful of is being clear on who has pickup duty. The worst thing is looking at each other in horror, visualizing one of our munchkins stranded as they wait by themselves on the verge of tears for a parent who screwed up their pickup schedule.

Wisdom Through Experience

There are so many things you learn along the way as a co-parent of divorce. New situations will come up and different issues will arise as children grow older. You can feel your out-of-control factor reaching new heights. You will feel like you are constantly being tested, but things will only become easier if you let go of your insecurity.

You have to come to terms with the reality that you *do* lose control when they are with their dad. Children will survive if they don't get your special preservative- and antibiotic-free hot dogs and the natural toothpaste from the health food store when they are at their dad's house. They do just fine on weekends of junk food and little sleep, so smile when he drops them off and say nothing.

When the door closes and I have my munchkins back to myself, I have learned to prepare myself for what I call the transitional witching hour. While they are happy to see me, it's hard for them to say good-bye to their dad. I try not to over hug or kiss them because they need to make their transition into a completely different environment.

Having dinner during the transition can feel like someone is missing. To make matters worse, I have to hear my kids grumble "I like it at Daddy's house better and I want to live with him forever because he is _____ or he has _____." I know some of this playing-one-against-the-other is normal and happens in nuclear families, it just cuts a little sharper when you are divorced.

This is when I take a deep breath and practice some extra patience and understanding. I'm able to keep my cool and not take it personally when I remember what the little guys have to go through and how hard it is for them. I have learned that my house will be utter chaos for a few hours until things settle down. When my kids are at their worst, I hug them and tell them I love them, which seem to diffuse some of their anxiety. Over time it has gotten better, but they still have their moments.

Overall, being a co-parent to your children with your ex requires a lot of patience, understanding, compromise and diplomacy to be successful. It will take time for all the pieces to fit together, but eventually they will. I like having my children grow up in an environment without fighting, tension or bad role-modeling. Divorce can be a great opportunity for children to learn. The best lesson is to show them that in bad situations, people can come together and make things work in a different way. Children are watching us all the time and learning; everything we do is role-modeling for them.

Divorce Culture and the Single Parent

Look around. Now that your marriage glasses are off, it's as if divorced families start coming out of the woodwork. At your neighborhood restaurant, you notice a single dad trying to keep his kids under control during his designated Thursday night out. You watch children getting picked up or dropped off for their visitation with the other parent, using McDonald's as common ground.

While at the park, you eavesdrop on an intriguing conversation between two divorced moms laughing about the dating world. Your information gathering session is interrupted by your children's excitement as they introduce you to their new friend Raquel, who lives in two separate houses with her mom and dad just like they do.

The most annoying thing is when acquaintances see your kid having a bad day or acting out. They look at you with pity in their eyes and make comments on how hard the breakup must be on the children. Who asked them anyway? I just smile and say sometimes it's just kids being kids. I have seen their rug rats act off the wall and these women are supposedly happily married, so what's their excuse?

I remember feeling like a character in the movie *Bye Bye, Love.* It's a great movie to rent that looks at the different journeys children and parents experience separately and together on their road to divorce recovery. There were so many times during the movie I thought, *Yeah, I remember going through that.* It will help you to laugh and have a little more heart when dealing with your own sometimes crazy reality. The movie gave great examples of what happens when the nuclear family changes into an adapted configuration.

What was once neat and compact has become complex, at times fun and sometimes hectic and messy. Suddenly there are many more cogs in the wheel that can create a variety of scenarios you never expected.

There are more people to deal with as parents find new partners and friends who might also have children. Your life suddenly changes with visitation schedules and new roles with your ex. I remember the first year being the most challenging, but then suddenly everything just started to feel like it was my new, normal life.

The Disneyland Dad

Dad is always the fun guy and Mom is always the heavy. This is a universal complaint women have whether they are married or divorced. The problem is that when you are divorced, this situation seems to be magnified. Dad gets them for a short amount of time and wants to make the most of it. Your children may be in a situation where Dad lavishes them with gifts, money, vacations and candy. You can start feeling bitter toward your ex and disconnected from your kids when they are away with Dad on some great adventure.

You probably can't compete with the energy or money he has for them, and you feel angry and insecure. Take a breath, if their dad is in their lives and giving them attention, it's great for your kids. As far as feeling like you can't compete, the great thing is that you don't have to. Children grow up and figure things out better than you think. As the primary caregiver, you are a constant they rely on to be there no matter what. While you might not be able to buy their first car or take them on a great vacation, they know how important you are to them. It's probably going to be you they come to when they have a problem they need to talk about.

Let them have a great time, and don't make them feel guilty for enjoying their time with their dad. When they come home and tell you how cool Dad is because they get to stay out late and eat whatever they wanted, *suck it up* and smile. Let them know that you are happy they had fun and that you are happy they are back home with you again.

While you probably spend more time with them, you are so occupied with homework and keeping them in line, you feel like you have to schedule fun on the list of things to do. Make an effort not to be all work and no play. Now would be a good time for you to take up a new hobby with your kids that can help you stay connected and be your special thing together. I know a mom who was able to find a tennis instructor who gave lessons in their neighborhood at a reasonable price. This was money well spent; years later they all play tennis together on the weekends and during family vacations. The friendly competition is great, and they really look forward to spending time together doing something that is fun and great exercise.

You don't need money to have fun and create memories with your children that will make all of you smile. More than anything, children want your time and attention. It doesn't have to be anything extravagant, a visit to a museum or park or a game of checkers can be magical. Anything you do with them will provide a real opportunity for communication and bonding. You might find out the most amazing things about them when you least expect it during casual conversation.

The most important thing is for you to be 100 percent focused on the fun of it. Kids know the difference, so don't give them half of your attention while you're busy doing something else that can wait. Shut the TV off and throw yourself in completely; it's not the quantity of time but the quality of time that is important. If you do little things with them, combined with plenty of hugs, kisses and kind words, your children will feel like they have everything they need from you and more.

From Pity to Party

That gaping hole you feel in your gut the first time your children leave your side to visit with their dad for the weekend can be painful. I remember the first hour or two being the most difficult. I actually tried to be productive by cleaning out their closet, which only bought me to my knees as tears welled up in my eyes. I smelled their clothes for any trace of kid scent; a bit melodramatic, yes, but I felt like wallowing in my own misery. When they finally returned, which seemed like an eternity, I hugged and kissed them until they were blue in the face. I couldn't stay away from them until my older son told me to get a grip.

I recovered until the first weeklong vacation they took without me. When they left I started having an intimate relationship with Ben and

Jerry's ice cream. I slipped into a deep depression and cried my eyes out into the wee hours of the night, channel surfing between Lifetime television and the Home Shopping Network. Not only did I get fat and puffy, I ran up quite the debt on my credit card in the name of immediate gratification. I was hosting and honoring myself in quite the pathetic little pity party with the theme of "It's my party and I'll cry if I want to."

The loss of control and distance away from them was very difficult. It took some time, but eventually I started finding better ways to utilize my free time. Out of necessity I had to get to the gym because my relationship with Ben and Jerry took its toll on my body. I couldn't get into my clothes, and I felt uncomfortable all the time. Working out was my saving grace because I was determined to get back in shape and it changed my focus. My attitude and perception about my situation started to change, and I started to put a different picture frame around my new life. I started feeling better about myself and more adventurous about doing fun things on my own.

I found comfort and humor in a strange phenomena that happened soon after the visitation schedule with their dad started. I call it "The Mommy Brigade." Many women from my child's preschool, who I barely knew, would stop me and report their findings of my ex interacting with my children. I was surprised that half of these women even knew that I was getting a divorce. It was like a secret alliance upon my behalf that got set up without my knowledge. Mere acquaintances would report back on how great he was with them in public as they provided positive commentary on how he held their hands when they crossed the street, how affectionate he was and how he properly disciplined them when they were out of control. They would continue on and tell me I had nothing to worry about and how lucky I was. They could never get a divorce because they would never trust their husbands to be such good fathers on their own. How bizarre! I have to admit that even though I knew my ex was an excellent father, I did find "The Mommy Brigade" reports reassuring.

Just like my attorney said, men who divorce and want to be with their children will rise to the occasion. At first, there is definitely a learning curve as they adjust to the responsibilities of being the single parent. Women have a much easier time because they are used to all of the responsibilities and sacrifices that come with parenting. For men, they have to take on a lot more than they did when they were in the marriage. After some time, they get the hang of it and their reward is a much closer bond with their children. I think most women don't give men enough credit; it's just a matter of adapting to a new situation and environment.

In time, you relax and realize your kids are in excellent hands. Suddenly your alone time does not have to be a miserable waiting game until your kids walk back through your door. You stop worrying and feeling sorry for yourself and realize the great opportunities this situation presents. It's almost like being a kid again, you can now start taking care of yourself and doing things you never had time for. This newfound freedom is so liberating and healing you will actually start to enjoy the sound of silence again.

It takes time to get used to that very lonely, empty, quiet feel of the house when it goes from being on wheels to complete silence in a matter of seconds. Sleeping alone at first is hard but when you wake up, the freedom factor kicks in and your time finally belongs to you. At first it seems strange and lonely, but then you start looking forward to some alone time to recharge your battery. You can pursue hobbies and romantic interests without cutting into your children's time.

After about a year, I worked up the courage to take a week vacation with my boyfriend while the children stayed with their dad. I had a great time away, and while my kids missed me, they had a great time at Disneyland with their dad. It got back to me that some miserably married old friends passed comments that I was a terrible mom because they would never leave their children in my situation. I had a good laugh over it—they were just jealous that I could and they couldn't.

Many women I interviewed said that once they had the courage to step out of their box, they used their free time without their children for things they always dreamed of doing. Here are just a few things they did: joined a book club, joined a wine club, took up a sport or hobby, took classes or a home study program to advance their education and earning potential, learned how to rock climb, took up bicycling, ceramics or sailing or, just relaxed at home and made time to meet friends and enjoy life.

It can be all about rediscovering yourself and finding the person you left behind. You no longer have to be the one whose needs are at the bottom of your list. You will learn to balance your life so there will always be time to take care of you and what makes your heart sing. Not only is this healthier, it makes you more attractive to others, including your children as you teach them to chase their own dreams and desires.

I remember an episode of *Dr. Phil* in which a single mother complained about her depression and anger when her children would leave her all alone for the holidays to visit their dad. This woman was devastated and stuck. Dr. Phil looked at her and asked her when she was going to make a choice to stop feeling sorry for herself. He started rattling off a list of productive, fun ways she could spend her time. She decided to take one of his suggestions and help out during Christmas at a homeless shelter. Without any expectations, this woman created a whole new network of friends who volunteered at the shelter. For years now she has considered these people her second family. She was only able to achieve this by letting go of her negative feelings and putting her energy toward helping others, which in the end wound up helping herself.

The Divorce Ripple Effect

Two people with children decide to end a marriage. The reaction is similar to what happens when you throw a stone into a still body of water. The ripple of water created starts slowly and spreads far and wide until the entire lake is moved by this simple action. The effects of divorce are very similar. You don't realize how many people's lives are affected by divorce, and how many more people you will now have to interact with. It's like anything else; you don't know what it's like until you have lived it for awhile.

When you ask yourself how this became your life, don't get all worked up into a lather, just take a deep breath and laugh when you can. The following are just a few examples of situations involving children that some women have found themselves in.

Who Would Have Thought?

- The suck-it-up motto is never so difficult to live by than when you have to deal with the very young woman who slept with your ex and broke up your marriage. Guess what, she is now taking care of your kids, and you have to work out scheduling their activities with her when you pick your children up at what used to be your house.
- Your own parents are now struggling with your new stepchildren. Suddenly, little people who are relative strangers are now running around calling them Grandma and Grandpa.
- Your child's best friend wound up in therapy for fear of abandonment after watching your family go through a messy divorce.
- You finally found the perfect guy until you realize he just doesn't get kids and doesn't want to. Suddenly you realize you're not just dating for you, but also for those precious little people waiting for you at home.
- Planning a romantic getaway with your boyfriend who is divorced with children is quite the chronological challenge. First of all, you have to hope your off weekends without children are in sync. To make matters interesting, in comes the ex-wife's boyfriend (who also has children), and he would like to take her on vacation. Try to stay with me. The problem is that this guy's ex's on/off weekend schedule does not coincide with her new boyfriend's children's schedule with their mother and she wants to flip weekends. Yikes! Way too many degrees of separation, but guess what, it's affecting your life and ability to take a vacation!
- You are feeling guilty when you realize your boyfriend's children will be at your house for the holidays and their mother is home alone. You feel guilty, but you just don't feel comfortable inviting her to your home.
- You are dating a man for a while who has a very good relationship with his ex-wife. His daughter is going off to summer camp and calls

to ask if we could meet her at the ice cream parlor to say good-bye before she leaves the next day. You pull up and realize her mom is there, which is fine because she is absolutely wonderful to you. What's not so fine is as you are all on line picking flavors, the ex-wife shoves her licked spoon into your boyfriend's mouth for a taste while you are standing right next to him. He looks right at you like a deer caught in the headlights. Hmmmm?

- You feel like the perfect nuclear family again as you take a vacation with your boyfriend's two kids when your children are with their dad for the weekend. Everything is great until the four-hour car ride home. Both kids go at it nonstop as you try to reason with them as your migraine intensifies and you finally lose it. When you finally get home and get out of the car, you realize you have fallen from your pedestal of camp counselor/cool girlfriend, to the bitch on wheels in just a few hours.

- You have to explain why your children's father now shares a bed with another man.

- You have a reunion with your ex's extended family a few years after the divorce that feels similar to a one-night stand. For some reason he can't make his grandmother's ninetieth birthday party. With short notice you get a call asking if you can come to the party with the children so they can surprise their great grandmother. You have little hesitation because she is a woman you continue to share a close bond with so you decide to deal with the strangeness of the situation and help make her day extra special. It's a surreal experience as you are greeted with big hugs and kisses. You all catch up on the last three years of your lives, and it's a great time. When it's time to go, there are promises of keeping in touch and sending photographs through the Internet, knowing full well it probably won't happen. It's like having a one-night stand with fifty people you used to be related to. It's great while it lasts, but you all know that it will probably be the last time you see each other.

- You walk into your child's preschool class to drop him off and are ambushed by the teacher. She tells you that she just realized that you are divorced, and what a shame it is because your ex is such a handsome man. You smile sweetly and tell her she can have him.

- You sense your children drifting away from you and actually have to work hard to stay connected to your kids when they are away on visitation and holiday with their dad.

- For about a month, your children tell you about a person who has a childlike nickname. You assume it is one of their playmates until you hear this character is now driving them somewhere in Daddy's car. After talking to some mutual friends, you realize that "Woogie" is actually your ex's new girlfriend, the same girl who used to babysit the children when you were married. Oh joy!!!

- Your teenage son is playing matchmaker for you with the teacher at school, and he is encouraging you to get out in the dating world. Once you decide to step out of your box, he is giving you fashion advice and coaching you on how to be cool. How did this happen, and how did we get here?

- You could actually form a closer bond with your children than you had before as a result of divorce.

- The woman who slept with your husband is now living with him and taking care of your children during visitations. There is now a second betrayal because she is crossing sacred ground once again. Your children report back that she lays in bed nestled next to them as she reads them a bedtime story. You have to *suck it up* and know that nobody could ever take your place as their mother. You can only hope that your ex would only let somebody in your children's life who was special and great with them. It still won't stop you from feeling violated, but if she is a good person and your children like her, count your blessings that she is not the Wicked Witch of the West.

- Your ex has married the Wicked Witch of the West. She is not very nice to your children, and you dread when their dad comes to pick them up as you helplessly wave good-bye. They come home unharmed and seem to have a closer bond with each other. They joke around and explain how they survived another episode of "Surviving the Step Monster" but had a good time with their dad.

Most mothers who I talked to said that as time moves on, your confidence in yourself and your co-parent grows as you both realize your children will be fine. Feelings of jealousy seem to lessen toward other people who are involved with your children. You come to realize that the more people in their lives who care for them the better. It just takes some patience and understanding for the new family configuration to settle down into a comfortable new place.

Their Future, Your Future

Try not to take yourself or the many situations you will experience too seriously. Growing up in divorce is not the worst thing that can happen to a child. The environment does have potential to set a child up for finding the negative or positive in life. You have an opportunity to help them learn and grow from a challenging situation. What it comes down to is you and how you handle whatever situation you find yourself in. As I said before, your children are watching your every move. How children turn out as a result of divorce will vary, depending mostly on their parents' attitudes and perceptions. The feelings and attitudes you have about life trickle down into your little ones' hearts and souls.

Find a way to forgive your ex and start a new relationship as co-parents—if not for yourself, then for your children's future. Many parents I spoke with said their transition out of the crazy circle of anger and resentment came with the help of an outsider. Sometimes it was a family member, friend, attorney (believe it or not) or a counselor. These people were able to help them get on a path to better serve their children. They were able to help the parents take the emotion out of a bad situation and find a way to create a new family configuration with low conflict.

At those times when you find yourself in total chaos, take a moment to sit down and breathe. Enjoy those priceless moments as you watch your children play, laugh and discover their world. It can almost be like a meditation that refuels your energy because it reminds you how simple and fun it can all be if you let it. When your little one comes into your room with a scissor and a chunk of hair in his hand that used to be on his head, take a time-out before you react. Use this moment to reminisce about your first hair-cutting adventure as a child. Try not to break out in laughter in front of your child for fear of more creative hair styling in the future. While children are an incredible amount of work and can stretch you to your limits, they will also be your saving grace.

I wish you and your adapted family a journey filled with adventure and hope. Find the help you need from your community, family and friends. Once you have found it, don't be afraid to ask for it when you need it.

Pay attention to the small miracles you'll find every day when you remember to sit down for some quality time with your children. Every day you have a choice to find the good or bad. Will you teach your children that the glass is half empty or half full? What choices will you now make for yourself and your children in your new world?

Time for You

Once you have your children squared away, it's time to talk about you. The experience of divorce changes who you are. When you are ready to start meeting new people and try dating again, it's like stepping out for the first time. The main and most important difference is that this time around, it's not just about you. There are little people waiting for you at home who need you to find a good match for them as well.

The next chapter will help guide you through the dating world. Get ready for some real life advice and laughter from many women and their adventures. You will learn about many things to try, to avoid and to enjoy. Take a deep breath and feel free to laugh; it's very healthy and very necessary.

Part Two

The Adventure
Finding Your Happily Ever After
(ad ven chur) n. an unusual and exciting experience

Dating and Sex: Ready, Set, Stop!

Okay, so you're sitting alone in your bed. You look to the other side only to be met with a vast, empty, cold space. Perhaps your soul is in need of companionship because you're lonely? Nope, that's not it. Wait—you notice a familiar stirring in your body that tells you it doesn't want somebody to talk to. It's interested in one thing and one thing only. That's right, it's screaming out for SEX, and it wants immediate gratification. At times like these I remember thinking to myself, *This must be what it feels like to be a guy—got to have it and don't care how I get it.* Hmmm. After taking a few slow, deep breaths, I started to analyze my new situation. Here I am, a nice Jersey girl who guarded her virginity until the age of twenty. When I got married a few years later, I discovered how much I truly enjoyed sex. Within the sacred institution called marriage, sex was a natural and worry-free way to express my love. Now I find myself separated and on the road to divorce. This new situation has not stopped my body from wanting to satisfy a natural desire that was fulfilled for over a decade. What's a girl to do?

Abstinence—with Toys

After a year of no sexual contact, I needed an outlet. I was past the stage of putting my sexual needs into hibernation. The bear woke up and she was very hungry. Just about any species of male was starting to look good to me. I started flirting with the guy making fresh sushi behind the seafood case at my local supermarket. I never knew a man creating sushi could be so sexy. I would watch as he gently but skillfully folded over a California roll inside out—and I was gone. *That's just great,* I thought, *now I'm finding food preparation erotic as I stand under the fluorescent lighting with my neighbors as they shop for produce. Can somebody please help me?*

What compounded my sex-deprived state even more was that the opposite sex was suddenly paying attention to me. How could this be? I just had the year from hell, I was exhausted all the time, and men find this attractive? Looking back, I was probably more attractive because of my newfound self-confidence. For years, my self-esteem was in the toilet and I was very unhappy. Making a choice to divorce and finally telling the world was like putting down a ten-pound bag of bullshit I had carried while pretending to be the "Barbie Doll" couple. The honesty was very liberating, and I felt excited about starting a new "true" life with endless possibilities.

The attention I was getting from men was very refreshing and enjoyable. I felt like I must be giving off some single sex pheromone that alerts the male species that a female is ready to mate! Guys were actually flirting with me, and I was not blushing but boldly smiling right back. I felt like a kid in a candy store, but one with the responsibilities of life and two beautiful children. Acting reckless and irresponsible was not an option at this point of my life. My unconscious solution to my recreational needs was to incorporate into my dreams old boyfriends and men who did work for me around the house. I was turning into quite the little Jezebel in my altered state of consciousness called sleep. I would wake up, look at myself in the mirror and chant "Get a grip." I knew changes had to be made before I did something I might regret. I needed time, space and relief, not a new relationship on any level so soon after ending one of twelve years.

At least I knew I was not alone. I remember a woman named Ellen telling me how hard it was adjusting to sleeping alone at night after her divorce. First, she was lonely and scared. Coming home to a dark, empty house was intimidating enough, but then she would get "spooked." A comprehensive search of the house included all closets, showers and beneath all beds to be sure the boogeyman was not lurking in the darkness.

Months went by until she calmed down enough to search only under her bed before shutting off the lights. After about six months of this silly ritual, she actually started hoping somebody was under her bed. Yikes! She searched for an old vibrator her ex-husband had bought for her years ago, much to her embarrassment. Ellen explained that she was always a bit shy and uncomfortable about the whole "sex toy thing," but now her only salvation was a small, battery-operated machine that buzzed. After searching for an hour with no luck, she wondered if her ex had taken the massager out of spite. Hmmm . . . she could almost hear him snickering.

That night out of desperation Ellen decided to open her mind and be creative. Instead of hunting down the nearest male species, she jumped onto the Internet. Within minutes she bought herself her very own vibrator. She said it was a breeze to find the perfect alternative that met all of her specifications after some careful, private research. She would have preferred clicking the perfect man into reality, but she knew that would always be a fantasy.

Ellen's vibrator became a close, personal and satisfying "fill in friend," and abstinence started looking like a good option. Becoming comfortable with masturbation was easy now that it was becoming so hip. Ellen felt like a woman of the new millennium who took matters into her own hands. She made a choice to stay safe and sane by satisfying her desires without the risk of getting a sexually transmitted disease or jumping into a relationship she wasn't ready for.

The addition of sex toys makes a life of abstinence more realistic. They provide a safe alternative to satisfy a very normal biological human urge that eventually must be satisfied. There are so many different products on the market that can fit everyone's pocketbook and palate. These wonderful pieces of equipment and machinery can help keep someone from getting intimate before they are ready, and when they are, sex toys are great to share. I started thinking that it's like putting someone on a diet. It's not possible to stop eating food so you offer healthier alternatives. The low-fat yogurt shake might not taste as good as a hot fudge sundae but can still be quite satisfying.

While masturbation is still a very private issue, people are getting more comfortable talking about it. This particular act got a lot of airtime—prime time on a popular HBO series called *Sex and the City*. The main characters of the show were women who talked regularly about how they spent their entire day pleasuring themselves—by themselves. The sexually liberated character Samantha was eager and proud to tell her girlfriends that the reason her complexion looked so fabulous was because she spent the day in bed masturbating. Charlotte (the goody two-shoes character) required an intervention by her girlfriends after she locked herself in her apartment for days with a certain vibrator following a horrible breakup with a man. She felt that she found the answer to getting her needs met minus the aggravation, ultimately making men obsolete. Miranda (the no-nonsense, professional yuppie) had trouble hiding her very necessary vibrator from her very nosy and judgmental housekeeper. How is it that Carrie, my favorite character, avoided this particular subject matter?

While channel surfing one night I saw two professional, attractive women discussing in great detail a variety of sex paraphernalia displayed on a table. One woman was a gynecologist, the other a sex therapist. The show was called *Berman & Berman*. I can't think of a better combination of professionals to educate me on the diverse products one can acquire to help achieve maximum overdrive.

After getting over the shock that I was watching a helpful review of different sex toys on TV, I started to choose which items I had to have. I've been "turned on" to this show ever since, and I have to say it provides great information on many women's health issues. I applaud them for being so brave and "on the edge" when addressing women's sexuality. They discuss some very personal issues that most women face and offer solutions and alternatives. How refreshing to get helpful advice rather than being told to ignore the problem and learn to live with it.

After all of this exposure to sexual satisfaction without getting any, I remembered that a friend of mine had a side business selling sex toys. A phone call later, I was scheduled to host something called a "Fuckerware Party." That's right, girlfriend—desperate times call for desperate measures.

No, we are not talking about a room full of women purchasing Tupperware or jewelry. What we are talking about are romantic lotions, potions and hardware that require batteries to "do things." Could this be the opportunity for the quick fix I was searching for? A few years earlier I would've been shocked, but I decided to step out of my box into my new life and live a little on the edge.

Three weeks later I hosted a party with approximately thirty very excitable women who marched through my front door with munchies, alcohol and plenty of cash. I knew it was going to be an interesting night when one of my closest friends came in with a fruit salad featuring bananas dressed in different colored condoms. The party started out a bit stiff and hesitant, but after some food and drink, the ladies were ready to get down and dirty. My hostess started her presentation, and after about a half-hour she crossed over from lotions, potions and powder to the show-and-tell hardware. She incorporated me into her schtick, which provided much entertainment for my friends as they watched me turn various shades of red.

An interesting transformation happened ten minutes after the hostess started presenting her goodies. Girls started taking notes as if in class and compared firsthand knowledge of things they already owned and would never part with. I felt like I had been living in a cave for the last ten years. The conversation became comfortable, funny and informative. We spoke with such ease that nobody would have believed the subject was sex toys; it was quite liberating. As her presentation was coming to a close, she saved the crème de la crème—the pièce de résistance—for the finale. She described a feeling that started from the core of the body, moved slowly but powerfully up and down every extremity into the fingers and toes to produce multiple explosive orgasms. We were all breathless as we watched her turn on and explain in detail this obscene piece of equipment that must have been designed by a woman. She added that this was the type of orgasm that comes along only once in a while when all circumstances are perfect. "But ladies," she stated, "it can be replicated any time you want, however many times you want; all you need to do is take home the Wascally Rabbit tonight." Immediately girls started to laugh as they raised their hands to confirm that every word she spoke was true.

One girl was brave enough to tell us a story that made us laugh so hard we cried. One night, when her children were at their dad's house, she felt a bit restless. She thought about how she might calm herself down when the Wascally Rabbit came to mind. She spent the night in her bed with her old reliable friend and woke up in the morning feeling refreshed and at peace. Running late for work, she ran out the door, forgetting that the big rabbit was still under her covers. Returning home after a full day, she came home to a clean house and a bed that was made. Every cell in her body freaked. She had forgotten that the maid was coming to clean and imagined the sight of this poor woman stripping the sheets from the bed. She wanted to die of embarrassment as she searched the bed for any possible sign of her friend, but he was gone. Mortified, she knew she had to confront the situation head on; the rabbit had to be rescued. She approached her housekeeper with a bright red face and apologized for what she left lurking in the bed. Without skipping a beat the woman from South America said, "Oh, don't apologize, it's perfectly natural. I have to say I have never seen one quite like that. Can you get me one?"

After two hours of order-taking, many a rabbit had new owners who were anxiously awaiting a quiet moment to experience the ultimate "O." At the end of the evening, my friend told me that her sales entitled me to over $250 worth of merchandise. Let's just say I had no problem spending it and, yes, my prize purchase was the Wascally Rabbit.

As I helped my hostess load her car with all of the "equipment and machinery," she started to laugh at me because she saw I was still a little shell-shocked by the whole sex toy party experience. She said it might make me feel better to know that the history of vibrators is chronicled in the medical books. They were actually used in the early 1800s to treat women who suffered from a condition known as "hysteria." The symptoms were anxiety, irritability and increased vaginal secretions— basically a cross between PMS and sexual arousal. I started laughing but she assured me that if I did some research I would be quite surprised. My education on the subject matter left me astonished.

Get this: A well-accepted and commonly used treatment in the 1600s for "hysteria" required doctors to use their fingers to stimulate the female patient's clitoris to orgasm! Yes, you read that sentence correctly. Unfortunately, this process was time-consuming, laborious and caused the poor physician's fingers to cramp up. As a solution to the doctor's dilemma, a fellow physician invented the first steam engine vibrator. Everyone was happy, the patients got buzzed to their delight and the money kept rolling in. For years, the vibrator enjoyed a "politically correct" status until the porn industry started using it in unacceptable sexual scenarios, resulting in its "back in the closet" status.

Only recently are vibrators becoming more mainstream in stores again, but under the guise of a "massager," never a vibrator. People seem to be more open about sex and what feels good. Maybe it's about the fitness craze or that we just need relief from a stressed-out world. I remember a scene from *Sex and the City* where Samantha (the sexually liberated character) marches into a Sharper Image–type store to return a nonvibrating vibrator. The salesclerk sneers at her that they don't sell vibrators at his store, only massage units, horrified at her insinuation. Samantha just laughs and asks for an exchange. While she's waiting, she notices three lost looking women timidly hovering over the table with the many different gadgets called "massagers." Unable to resist the opportunity to "educate" them, Samantha proceeds to give the women a crash course on the pros and cons of each unit and the best way to use each for maximum satisfaction. They are grateful for the guidance and become bolder in their hunt for the perfect buzz.

I'd like to conclude the vibrating subject matter by saying I have had the Wascally Rabbit experience. In my opinion, every woman should have at least one experience in her lifetime with this wonderful piece of equipment. Although there will never be a replacement for the real thing, this is a very, *very* good alternative.

I walked away from my little sex toy party feeling quite liberated and normal. It was such a relief to talk to other women so easily about sex and what makes them and their significant others feel good. We all shared excellent stories, techniques and fantasies that helped spark our imaginations in our own lives. What I wasn't expecting was a very serious talk with a dear friend who wanted to discuss sexually transmitted diseases. She said after watching her friend's reckless sexual behavior after divorce, she wanted to make sure I would start off my new life using my head.

Jillian—43 years old

I remember feeling like a fish caught in a fishbowl when I first started dating. You know the neighborhoods that have signs depicting people peering through binoculars with the words CRIME WATCH underneath? Well, keep the picture but underneath put the words SLUT WATCH—that's how it was in my neighborhood. Everybody had to know my business. The questions were nonstop: "Whose car was in your driveway?" "Was that a new guy I saw walk out of your house?" "Hey, it looks like you're getting some pretty good action over there!"

The gossiping was incredible, and I knew they thought the worst of me. Yes, I dated different people, but there were also a lot of men who were just friends or relatives who would stop by for dinner. People love to make up stories out of nothing, especially when they are jealous and have no lives. The thought of moving to make a new start and get away from the nosy neighbors was very tempting, but it was too inconvenient for my family. I learned to be more discreet and developed a thicker skin. Eventually I became old news and people moved on to gossip about the next scandal.

Looking back at the early stages of my dating experience, I was a bit of a crazy woman. I have a high-powered job with a big company that requires me to travel quite a bit in a private jet. I developed a split personality for awhile. When I was at work, I was this confident, cocky, man-eating woman. My divorce resulted from infidelity on my husband's part, and I was feeling very burned. It was as if I were out on a mission to prove my sexuality and desirability to the opposite sex. I was a corporate big shot not looking for a relationship, just power and good sex.

When all I was looking for was a one-night stand, it was "raining men, hallelujah." Not only did they want my sex, but they wanted me and practically begged for my phone number. Ironically, when I came home it was a completely different story. I was a mommy in my small town who just wanted to find a nice guy I could settle down with. I could barely get a date, let alone hold a guy's interest for more than two minutes if I was lucky. At home I felt desperate and insecure. My needing and wanting to find the right guy was like man repellent.

Once I stepped back and looked at what was happening, I realized how important confidence was when trying to meet a man. I looked the same at home and work, outside of the clothing, but clearly the discrepancy arose from how I felt in different environments and what I projected. I might have acted confident and put together on the outside, but inside I was a wreck both at work and home. I guess I was just a great actress at work. It was clearly time to work on my self-esteem.

It took awhile for me to blend the confident corporate babe with the sweet mommy type who wanted a solid relationship. The process of healing and acting took about a year of "taking a walk on the wild side," but I finally settled down into a new and better place. When I think back to all the chances I took with unsafe sex and situations, a shiver runs up my spine. I feel very lucky to *have emerged intact and healthy.*

There is a happy ending. I got my life together with the help of a good therapist and spent some time just being alone. When I started dating again, I had a new perspective on what I needed and the types of guys who interested me. It was no longer the good-looking, macho, controlling type I was interested in, but a guy who would prove to be a "diamond in the rough." I found a sweet, kind, wonderful man, and when he kissed me, my knees weakened and I turned to mush. After much trial and error, I found a great friend and a great lover in one package—I never knew that was possible.

Lessons Learned

- Be prepared for the gossip mill. The stories that get back to you will make your head spin and might be miles from the truth. Learn to laugh and realize that the source of the gossip is people who are bored and miserable with their own lives.
- Don't be reckless after your divorce. Get an education about sexually transmitted diseases and the best ways you can protect yourself.
- Time alone can be healing and important to work on your self-esteem and find yourself again. If you get too restless, buy yourself a really good vibrator.

Sex and Safety: A Wake-Up Call

A few days after that crazy party, my friend and I got together for dinner to have that woman-to-woman chat. She revealed a secret she had kept from me for years. She had been married for the last eight years to a wonderful man and had been trying to have a baby for the last three years. I knew about her battle with infertility but I never knew the real cause. She revealed that she had contracted chlamydia when she was dating, many years prior to her marriage. She was asymptomatic for a while until it progressed to something called pelvic inflammatory disease (PID), which eventually led to her infertility problems.

I felt like crying for my friend's pain and bad luck; girls like her are not supposed to get sexually transmitted diseases. Who was I kidding—I knew better than that—but it was just hitting too close to home. My friend explained that she let me in on her secret because she wanted me to get a reality check on STDs and reinforce the importance of safe sex before I went out into the dating world.

We continued talking and she had another story about a friend with whom she went to college. This girl got herpes from the very first lover she had at the age of twenty-one. What was very disturbing to me was how she contracted the virus. As a primary health care provider, I considered myself knowledgeable enough about STDs until I heard this information. My friend explained to me that her friend contracted the virus from her boyfriend when he was completely asymptomatic and he was wearing a condom.

I almost fell off my chair. If there were no lesions or symptoms and he was wearing a condom, what was I missing? What I learned is that somebody with herpes can spread the virus through their skin without evidence of symptoms or lesions. This can happen many times over the course of a year, making the virus contagious even when it looks and feels safe. The incredible part is that it spreads from all over the genitalia, including the scrotal region and buttocks. Putting a condom on the shaft of a penis only protects a third of the area, leaving the rest of the genital region exposed for transmission from one person to another. You can never get enough protection from this virus unless the entire pelvic region is wrapped in latex.

Alec Baldwin was being interviewed on TV about venturing off into the dating pool after his divorce. He said, "What do you have to do nowadays before you sleep with somebody, boil them and bag them?" At first I thought *how crude;* now I'm thinking, *how true.* My ignorance was very disturbing to me, which made me wonder about the public's knowledge regarding STDs, and what they knew and thought about protection.

When I talked to my single friends, they were resistant to talking about the subject. They said they knew what they needed to know about STDs, and as long as they used a condom and felt comfortable with their sex partner they were perfectly safe. After a few more questions, it was clear to me that they had minimal knowledge and very little dialogue with their doctors on this topic. Unfortunately, it's not until problems arise that a patient gets more of an education than they ever expected; too little, too late.

While men suffer from STDs, a woman's anatomy makes her more vulnerable to symptoms and complications. Some STDs can be asymptomatic, and if left undetected and untreated can cause lifelong complications and possibly death. Women can suffer from PID, sterility and cancer.

For instance, the primary cause of cervical cancer is HPV, human papillomavirus, which is a very common STD. Clinical symptoms may be venereal warts on the outside genitalia but most of the time women will be asymptomatic. If a woman has a strain of HPV that is high risk, there is a high likelihood she will develop cervical cancer. The good news is that when HPV is detected through routine tests, your doctor will determine the best treatment and a follow-up care plan to prevent you from getting cervical cancer.

Lessons Learned

- GET REGULAR PAP SMEARS, LADIES. THEY CAN SAVE YOUR LIFE!

Stacey—34 years old

When I was in college I had a brush with a sexually transmitted disease. I was lucky because my treatment only required an antibiotic and, within a couple of weeks, I was completely cured. That experience changed my attitude toward sex, safety and respecting my health. I was always careful when picking my sexual partners and insisted on always using a condom.

When I got engaged a few years later, I insisted that my future husband and I get tested for STDs. While he wasn't crazy about the idea, I reminded him how great sex would be without a condom. Without hesitation, he picked up the phone to make our appointment. We both tested free of any sexually transmitted diseases and celebrated that weekend in bed. The next year we were married, and seven years later we separated when I found out he was having an affair. My first call was not to a lawyer but my ob-gyn to get tested. Luckily, I came back negative for any STDs and within a year I was divorced.

It took me about a year to jump back into the dating pool. After a few months of blind dates, I found a great guy I met at the gas station, of all places. After the third date, things started getting hot and heavy. I told him that I wanted to take things slow and get to know each other better before getting intimate. He agreed and was very patient with me, which made me fall in love with him. After about two months, I was the one ripping his clothes off and begging him for sex, which caught him by surprise.

There was not a condom in sight, which put a screeching halt to a much-needed romp in the bedroom. We were desperate; within minutes, we were in the car making a mad dash for the nearest drugstore to stock up on supplies. During the car ride we had time to cool down and started to have "the talk" about safe sex. We shared our sexual histories and I explained that if we were ready to become sexually active, I wanted both of us to get tested. He asked me if it was really necessary because he felt healthy and knew I was safe, having had recent tests. I told him it was a deal breaker and he agreed.

When it came to making the appointment he had a moment of panic. He wondered what would happen if he actually had something. There would be an official record of it, and people at his office might find out because the staff handles his insurance and disability policies. I understood his possible predicament and had an idea. We should both go to a clinic and pay with cash. He thought that was a good idea but wanted to go under a different name just for extra privacy. We made the appointment, but when they called his alias name, he did not respond. I had to give him a little push until he realized and we laughed about the whole situation.

We went in together, and, to his surprise, the panel of STD testing was more extensive than he expected. It included: HIV, gonorrhea, herpes, chlamydia, hepatitis B and C, and syphilis. We agreed to do all of them—better safe than sorry. My boyfriend almost ran out the door when the nurse explained that to test for chlamydia in a male, she has to stick a small tube inside his urethra through his penis by about an inch. She reassured him that it would only pinch for a second; he looked at me as all the color washed out of his face. I told him it was his choice, if he always wanted to wear a condom it was okay with me. He decided to live through the temporary discomfort, and within seconds it was over.

We got our results back a couple of weeks later. I tested negative, and he tested positive for hepatitis B. I don't know who was more horrified. He was in denial and asked them for a second test, which came back positive. I watched him break down in tears and disbelief. The doctor explained that many people have the virus and are walking around asymptomatic. His mind became like a Rolodex of all of his sexual partners; he couldn't think of one incident where he could have contracted it.

The doctor had us both in for a consultation on how to manage the virus and protect against further spread. I was a wreck; I narrowly escaped getting a serious STD twice in my life. Now I was in love with someone with hepatitis. Part of me wanted to run, but I couldn't. This man was wonderful to me and I empathized with his situation because I had been there and knew what it felt like. The doctor gave us a helpful video to review and get a better understanding of the virus. It was a documentary of people living with the virus and how they overcame obstacles on their own and with their partners.

I've been married to this man for the past five years. We have a great relationship and practice safe sex with a condom and I remain uninfected. He has had no symptoms and appears to be a carrier of the virus. We use the necessary precautions, but we hardly think about it anymore.

I am so grateful we tested for STDs. It gave me the opportunity to make a choice of staying or leaving the relationship. If we did not do the testing and I contracted hepatitis, I would have had too much anger toward myself and my partner. I am well aware of the chance that I am taking, but it is an informed choice. From my experience I learned that anyone out there is susceptible to an STD, and some diseases are worse than others. I was not about to throw out a beautiful relationship over a virus. If, in the end, I contract hepatitis, it's the calculated risk I have taken for love, and I am at peace with my decision.

Lessons Learned

- THERE IS NO SUCH THING AS SAFE SEX, ONLY SAFER SEX!
- Some STDs are without symptoms; having a heart-to-heart talk with a potential sex partner about their sexual history can be a waste of time.
- Get the following blood work and tests done on you and your love interest before your clothes come off: herpes, gonorrhea, chlamydia, hepatitis B and C, syphilis, and HIV. Ask your doctor if there is any updated testing you should know about.

Your Sexual Survival IQ

We teach our children sex education in school, but adults could use some major updated information through continuing education classes. AIDS is a very serious disease almost everybody thinks about when practicing safe sex, but, as you've learned, it's not the only one to be concerned about. There are more common STDs out there that can result in lifelong complications and also become fatal. The public needs to become more active in getting updated information through their doctors and public clinics. A new awareness can save lives and prevent the epidemics we are currently facing, which is more serious than most of us want to believe.

Take the following test and check your *Sexual Survival IQ*.

1. Herpes can be transmitted by the following acts when one partner is a carrier of the virus but displays no sores or signs of an outbreak:
   a. vaginal intercourse with a condom
   b. oral sex
   c. rubbing genitals together without intercourse
   d. anal intercourse with a condom
   e. all of the above
   f. none of the above

2. The virus chlamydia can be asymptomatic and result in sterility in women when left untreated. What percentage of the female population will acquire the virus in their lifetime?
   a. 20%
   b. 50%
   c. 15%
   d. 75%
   e. 5%

3. True or False: Hepatitis can be transmitted by all of the following acts:
   a. vaginal or anal intercourse without a condom
   b. hand to genital contact
   c. using your boyfriend's razor or any other personal hygiene items
   d. oral sex
   e. sharing sex toys

Answers: 1. E, 2. D, 3. True

If the correct answers sent a shockwave through your system, I urge you to read up on STDs. Unfortunately, most of us are walking around with a false sense of security, thinking that safe sex simply requires the use of a condom and an HIV test.

This information is presented to remind you to do the best you can to protect yourself once you step back into the dating world. Learning about STDs should not make you fearful of sex but empower you with knowledge. Your sexual behavior is the key to keeping your body healthy as you enter the dating world. Don't be scared. Get out and discover yourself again, and have fun and be safe.

For those of you who are already infected with an STD, information is available to help you discuss the situation with a potential sex partner and the best ways in which you could protect them from transmission. (Visit my Web site *www.todaysdivorcedwoman.com* for more information.)

The Dating Circus: A Critical Review

Now that you have the necessary information it's not time to go home and hide under the covers. No way, baby, carpe diem! It's time to be bold and start a new adventure armed with information, a new attitude and a little toy. While it's not a good idea to lock yourself in your room and have a strictly monogamous relationship with your new sex toy, it's not a bad idea to make an occasional date with it.

Do you remember the movie *There's Something About Mary*? If you haven't seen it, go out and rent it and get ready to laugh. There is a part in the movie where a guy finally gets his chance to date his dream girl. His best friend advises him on how not to blow the opportunity. His primary suggestion was to relieve his manly urges by himself with a girly magazine right before going out on the date. (For those of you who know the movie, I'm sure you're recalling that most disgusting hair gel scene, but you can't stop yourself from having a chuckle.)

His friend's reasoning was that when a man relieves himself, he is capable of normal human contact and conversation. Going into a date with a loaded gun could result in possible horn dog behavior. To attempt winning the woman of his dreams, he must not be ruled by his penis; it's best to tame the beast before any female interaction. The process of relieving himself would render him calm and able to have an intelligent conversation—the ultimate first fantasy date for a woman. I think the same scenario can play out for women when they are totally ruled by their sexual urges, preventative measures may be necessary.

Lessons Learned

- When going out on your first few dates, if your libido is out of control, get a handle on it. A visit with your favorite buzz might be the best thing to stop you from jumping into someone's bed too soon just to get some satisfaction.

Calling All Single People

There is reason to rejoice, there has never been a better time to be single. Single living has become hip as the "traditional family" is no longer the norm because people are choosing to fly solo. Some say we are approaching the day when the United States will be an unmarried majority nation.

Some of the factors causing the change are a high divorce rate, self-sufficient women, fear of making a mistake and more focus on career. Reflective of our society's evolution is the popularity of the show *Sex and the City*, registries for singles for housewarming and birthdays at stores like Williams-Sonoma, and the breakup of our celebrated icon couple, Barbie and Ken.

After forty-three years, Barbie and Ken hit the skids. The vice president of Mattel stated that Barbie had had enough of Ken's broken promises. His inability to find a career outside of looking pretty in his Speedo and sitting on lounge furniture was about all she could take. She was also very frustrated with their inability to produce offspring because Ken apparently only comes in a box.

As a self-sufficient career woman, Barbie's future possibilities are endless. Maybe she will become a single mother by cloning herself in a child she affectionately calls "Mini Barbie." Perhaps Barbie will choose to trade in Ken for Midge, and embark on a same sex union. With some luck, we may see Barbie wear one of her many wedding gowns to her legal lesbian wedding.

The point is that we are living in a brave new world where divorced women are a segment of the population that is wading, swimming and diving into a dating pool filled with single people. The transformation is helping the divorced woman feel less intimidated and ostracized by her social status. The shy girl no longer has to feel like she is alone or odd girl out on Saturday night with all of her married friends. The in-between stage of finding yourself before finding your soul mate is no longer a waiting game filled with sadness and isolation. Singles are out there celebrating social lives that are filled with friends and lovers as they enjoy their journey and search for "the one" without compromising on what they need.

Female friends can be found at the local divorce support group. Most groups have great programs that divide individuals into the stage of divorce they are in, which helps deal with specific issues. Many women said they made lifelong friendships in a nonthreatening environment that gave them tools to live through the process and afterlife of divorce.

The Internet, dating services, religious institutions, and clubs for sports and special interests have always been great options for singles young and old. What's interesting and exciting are the new groups and venues that are being created to satisfy the growing market of singles who enjoy their freedom but are still open to finding their soul mate. Sasha Cagen is the author of a great book called *Quirkyalone: A Manifesto for Uncompromising Romantics*. She has recently organized the first Quirkyalone International Day, celebrated in big cities across the nation. Ironically, the day of the gathering was Valentine's Day. The author created a space for singles that "resist the tyranny of coupledom in favor of independent self-expression." This new environment we are living in helps every type of personality feel more comfortable as they take a leap of faith back into single living and loving again.

Am I Ready to Date?

How do you know when you are ready to start dating? Listen to your gut and that little voice inside your head that speaks the truth. The problem is that we have to be brave and strong enough to hear it and then listen to what it tells us to do. (I wonder how many of us would have gotten married if we had paid attention to that little voice.) Some people say that you shouldn't even consider dating until one year after your divorce becomes final. First of all, that could take years, and secondly, everyone has their own unique set of circumstances. This is not a timetable or cookbook call, it's one of those decisions you make along the way.

If the answer is that you are ready, you should have a clear idea of what you want and don't want in your next relationship. You should have had enough time to reflect on what went wrong in your marriage and how you intend to improve your communications and actions for a healthier, happier union in the future.

That old cliché is true; you have to be happy on your own before you can be happy in a relationship. This requires you to have a healthy mind, body and spirit with a good handle on your finances and career. Walking into a new situation with the knowledge that you can stand on your own two feet will be a great boost to your self-esteem and sanity, but more importantly, it will help you see things more clearly and calmly. Get your life together before you get serious with somebody. With that said, there is no reason why you can't dip your feet in and just have some fun again. Slow down, enjoy your new single status and take your time, but don't waste your time.

Speaking of not wasting your time, what are the best ways to meet potential mates for your new life? The saying "You have to kiss a few toads before you find your prince" is unavoidably true, but how can we minimize some of the misery and maximize the fun? Getting back into the single scene is a combination of excitement and nausea at the same time. The main thing to remember is to have a good attitude about going out to meet another person. If there is no love match, you might have found a friend plus had the chance to practice your people skills. The worst-case scenario is that you have a funny story to tell your friends and be able to laugh a little at the whole process. Remember that this is a journey and it may take time, so when you feel a bit jaded, readjust your attitude and put a smile on your face because you never know what is behind the next door.

Hannah—35 years old

When I got married at the tender young age of twenty-seven, I had no clue as to what I was getting into. Everything looked great on paper or so I thought: same age, same religion, same profession, same life plan that included children, both athletic, great chemistry in the bedroom and we were in love. If it were only that simple. Unfortunately, that beautiful package was missing the two critical components, compatibility and friendship!

Looking back at our engagement, I now see that the writing was on the wall. When we were not making love, we were fighting like cats and dogs. More red flags started flying when I realized he had a horrible relationship with his family. I tried to break off the relationship a few times, but I just wasn't strong enough or brave enough to listen to my inner voice. The night before my wedding, I slept at my parents' house. My dad saw that I was uneasy and persuaded me to spill my guts about all my doubts. With less than fifteen hours before the big wedding day, he sat up with me and listened. In the end he told me not to worry about the money; if I didn't want to get married, it was okay with him. What an angel!

I decided to go through with the marriage, and the next morning I sat in the limo unable to move. My entire wedding party waited on the curb patiently as I tried to analyze my intense nausea, wondering if this was just normal cold feet or a real gut feeling telling me to RUN. After about twenty minutes of sentimental tears and stalling, my father said it was time to go. I looked at him and asked him what advice he could give me, as I was about to start my new life. He smiled at me and said in a very sweet yet comical voice, "Get the fuck out of the car." One hour later I was married.

We had a few moments of good over a decade but the bad tipped the scales significantly. We both tried to save the marriage at different times but very rarely were we working together. After fighting the good fight for years, we were both miserable, we both wanted out and one of us had to put an end to our misery. At the end of the day, I was the one to pull the plug; a move for which *my ex-spouse will never forgive me because he lost control of the situation. What resulted was a messy, costly divorce that was fueled by anger and lasted over two years. The only parties that benefited from the mess were the fat-cat lawyers.*

I was a stress monster during post-separation, as my children and I transitioned into a new way of life. Compounding the stress were my dealings with attorneys and the outrageous fees draining my bank account. My body and psyche were taking a beating. I was letting the situation get the best of me, which resulted in weight loss, hair loss and insomnia. I was allowing myself to be consumed by the process.

A few months after my separation, I was in the neighborhood where my girlfriend worked and I stopped in to say hello. As I held my two-year-old on my lap, she asked me if I was ready to start getting a life. She was being brutally honest with me when she told me I looked like shit and that I needed to get a grip. It was a reality check because it made me realize I was living in my cave of misery and self-pity, which was probably affecting my children. She asked me if I was ready to start meeting some new people and possibly start dating. I just laughed and said, "No, thank you." Then she asked me if I was ready to have a little fun and have somebody tell me I look pretty. Without a second of hesitation, I smiled and said, "Oh, yeah." Within a minute she introduced me to her male associate who told me he had "just the guy" for me. I began wondering what I got myself into.

About a week later, while I was in the middle of refereeing my two little boys, the phone rang. A strange male voice was on the line, and I prematurely assumed it was another telemarketer. I responded rudely by saying, "Who are you and what do you want?" He responded calmly by stating his name and telling me that he had gotten my number from my friend. As my brain processed the information, I felt like such a buffoon and tried to cover up with a joke and sincere apology. Luckily he had a sense of humor and decided to ask me out on a date.

After rummaging through my closet, I settled on the third outfit my babysitter encouraged me to wear. It was a bit sexy, but classy and I felt good in it. I stepped into my heels, kissed my kids goodnight and off I went. The nausea and butterflies (in a good way) started the moment I got into my car. It was my first big, brave step to get myself back into life again. I was starting to remember that being happy and having fun is so much better than wallowing in self-pity.

I arrived on time and sat at the bar of a very chic restaurant we had decided on. The bartender was very friendly—too friendly—until I told him I was waiting for my date to arrive. Fifteen minutes later I was still sitting alone, milking my glass of Merlot. Bored and annoyed, I struck up a conversation with the hostess. I told her this was my first blind date after leaving my marriage. A cute waiter and my nosy bartender got wind of the story, and I became the pet project of the evening. The bartender gave me an escape route through the side entrance if my proposition turned out to be scary. The hostess was on the lookout, peering through the wood blinds on the window and waiting to give me the thumbs up or thumbs down. Finally, we have a suspect. The hostess reported back to me that he was driving a BMW. "Who cares?" I told her. "What does he look like?" I should mention that the hostess was about twenty, blond and beautiful. When she responded that he was a "hottie," I had reason to be excited.

A moment later, in walked my blind date—a bit older, and sexy, with a good smile and a warm handshake. My friendly bartender was looking very disappointed. We immediately clicked *and there was major chemistry between us. The nervous, sexual energy that was flying around the bar made me feel like a school-girl again. The hour we spent together made me euphoric and exhausted at the same time. The best part of the date for me was that there was no kiss goodnight, but a hug that let me know I was about to embark upon an adventure with this man.*

Lessons Learned

- When it comes to marriage, love and attraction are not enough. Try to find somebody you can be friends with first and then lovers.
- One of the first questions to ask a guy is to describe the relationship he has with his family and how he feels about his mother.
- The process of divorce can take time so you have to learn to find some comfort in the temporary discomfort. Once you start to laugh and have fun again, everything will improve.

When you are ready to date, how can you find the right doors to open? Women who seemed to have the most satisfaction in the dating arena followed this basic game plan.

The "Meat Market" Strategy

- Prince Charming is not ransacking the neighborhood knocking on doors, trying to find the perfect match for that magical glass slipper. However, the sisters are out there and the competition is fierce. If you want to see some action, you are going to have to step out of your comfort zone and get in the game of life.

- Treat your personal life more like you would handle a business. Ask yourself if this guy is a good "investment" of your time and energy; if not, cut bait and move on to the next prospect. Pure "carnal desire" is delicious but will not maintain its intensity in the long run; friendship will. Remember, "A kiss is just a kiss," but really liking and respecting a potential mate and wanting to jump his bones at the same time, now that's something. When considering a long-term "investment," look at the entire package and associated baggage. Blending works better when you have common values and interests. But don't forget his family and friends. If they make you want to run for the hills, RUN. Trust your instincts, but remember everyone's family is a little nuts.
- The biggest turn-on is a confident babe; any scent of desperation or insecurity is like man repellent. If your self-esteem is in the gutter, start doing the work you need to improve your mind, body and spirit; until then, put your best game face on and walk the walk.
- Stop obsessing about finding "the perfect guy" and chill out. Get involved in things that you enjoy such as cooking, hiking, ceramics and wine tasting. Chances are you will have a great time and meet new friends who share similar interests. People always say they find their mate when they weren't looking, so focus on your life and what makes you happy. Remember that happy is very hot!
- Safety first, girlfriend. Always keep the first date short and sweet; for instance, meet for coffee or a drink in a crowded area. If the guy is not your type or gives you the "heebie-jeebies," your torture is minimized to thirty minutes or less. If the date goes well, you can arrange dinner plans for the follow-up and then spend more time getting to know each other. Always let somebody know where you are going and when you will be back so they can check that you made it home safely.
- THERE IS NO SUCH THING AS SAFE SEX, only safer sex, and a condom is not enough.
- KEEP YOUR SENSE OF HUMOR!

> *Some men are like martinis, dry, very cold and they*
> *think they are fabulous because of the two olives*
> *dangling down at the bottom of their swizzle stick.*
> —Diane Farr

Here is a helpful review of the dating scene from the high-tech computer world to the old-fashioned matchmakers.

The Internet

The Good
- Inexpensive, on average about $12 to $100 a month.
- Safe, because you are anonymous until you decide otherwise (then you are on your own).
- Fun once you find the site that matches your needs. Shop around before you commit and try to find one that will narrow the playing field to your specifications and allow you the most freedom to communicate.

The Bad
- There is no screening so you never know who you might get.
- People lie, lie and lie. Someone who advertised himself as successful and the George Clooney type looks more like Woody Allen and lives in his parent's basement. This problem is common for both sexes.
- Some sites make it difficult to communicate by limiting the number of characters when typing.
- When you finally find what looks like a good match, making contact is impossible because the person is listed as inactive.

The Picks

eHarmony.com is a great site because it goes beyond the superficialities of focusing on looks, profession and money. The company delivers more than just a paragraph and a picture. An in-depth personality profile developed by a doctor delves into matching traits and values to help get a good, solid match. This is a little more costly than most Internet dating sites but worth it. Their logo is "fall in love for the right reasons."

The Matchmaking Services

Shop around and do your research to find a company that has a good reputation and can provide several references upon request. Check with the Better Business Bureau to make sure nobody has filed any complaints against the company or actual matchmaking person. This service can be expensive, starting from $600 to thousands of dollars. Read the contract carefully before signing and know what you are getting into. Find out if there is a way to get a refund if you are not satisfied with the service. While there are some very reputable matchmakers in the business, buyer beware of the person who feeds on desperate women by making unrealistic promises. Make sure that during your interview process you are very specific about what you are looking for so your time and money won't be wasted on inappropriate dates.

The Good

- Great for people who have no time to socialize and can afford to let someone do the work for them.
- If you like having control and don't mind spending the extra time, some companies allow you to pick your own dates by viewing photographs, videos and profiles.
- If you prefer to have someone else do all the leg work and don't mind relinquishing control, there are matchmakers who simply call you with a name, place and time to meet.
- A good way to free up your time and energy by allowing someone else to narrow down the playing field for you.

The Bad

- Expensive.
- Can be difficult to weed out the good companies from the bad.
- Most services do not provide background checks on the people with whom they are setting you up. Always remember that anyone can lie about who they are and what they do.
- Some contracts might lock you in, even if there are no suitable matches for your criteria.
- The sales pitch can be a hard sell so be objective and don't get caught up in the moment. Don't sign the contract until you are sure, no matter what extras they throw in. Chances are they will sign you up in the near future for the same package, so take your time and check out their competition.

The Picks

- IT'S JUST LUNCH—A staff member will set you up on forty-five-minute lunch dates after conducting a one-hour interview to determine what type of match they believe would be suitable. Most of the clients have either a college degree or advanced degree.
- GREAT EXPECTATIONS—You work together with the staff to find a match after you view hundreds of photographs, videos and profiles of eligible dates.
- RELIGIOUS MATCHMAKERS—If religion is important to you, this is a good place to look for a wide selection of eligible men.

Do-It-Yourself Method

If you are not comfortable paying for someone to help you find a mate, and the bar and club scene isn't your thing, it's time to take matters into your own hands.

- Be a good networker and let family and friends know that you are ready to start dating; don't be shy about it. One of the better ways to meet someone is by introduction, and it costs nothing.
- If the blind date well is running dry, get out and try something different; take a class that interests you, such as art or cooking.

- If you are the outdoors type, join a club for hiking, biking or fitness. You will get a great workout, feel good about yourself and get to meet new people alfresco.
- For the indoor types, check out the scene at local markets, bookstores, spas, meditation workshops and so on.
- The most important thing to do is "step outside of your comfort zone." Do things that challenge your mind and body and make you better as a person.
- If you happen to stumble on a potential suspect who looks good to you, don't wait for him to sweep you off your feet. It might be very uncomfortable, but try to make the first move by just saying "hello."
- Fear of rejection is what keeps most of us from moving forward, so get over yourself and be brave. The worst thing that can happen is a slight sting resulting from his lack of interest. Brush it off and move on because the positive interactions will more than make up for the occasional rejection.
- Remember Babe Ruth? Success is moving from one failure to another without giving up until you succeed.

Marcy—26 years old

I got married to a man who was my best friend for most of my life. The fact that we rarely had sex or kissed on the lips seemed inconsequential until I found him in our bed with another man. Was I disgusted and shocked? Yes. Was I surprised? No. I remember conversations we had had, where I expressed my sexual needs and desires. His answer was to buy me the best vibrator on the market and a monthly romp in the bedroom after we shared a bottle of wine.

The sight of two penises in my bed was just the thing I needed to leave a marriage where my husband should have simply stayed my best friend. Feeling drained and exhausted from the lie we were both living, I escaped to Italy on my dream vacation with a girlfriend with whom I grew up. I remember feeling very restless and sexually starved on the plane ride over the Atlantic. I had time to reflect on my life and my marriage, and how incredibly stifled I had felt for the last few years.

I had very little relationship experience or sexual history before my marriage, and then I entered into a sexless union. To compensate for my lack of action, I developed an imagination for sexual fantasy that got more creative as the years went on. I was the producer, director and actress of the best porn film that would never be made. A smile came across my face because suddenly I realized my new life was about to start, and I was going to make sure it was an adventure, starting with my Italian adventure. I promised myself I would be safe and smart, but unafraid to jump into life. Controlling the passion that burned inside me was going to be a challenge but I felt like a cat ready to pounce on the next available heterosexual male.

No sooner did I have this revelation than an opportunity presented itself as my friend and I were checking into our hotel. This beautiful Italian man approached me and introduced himself in broken, Italian-accented English that made my knees weak. I knew this could be trouble, but how could I resist! Next thing I knew we were sharing espresso and cannoli in an outdoor café. I learned that he was a successful artist here on business, showing his art at a local gallery. Things moved rather quickly from there. The next day I viewed his etchings, and that night I sat across from this hot Italian man at a very romantic restaurant—alone. The language barrier made it difficult to have any really in-depth conversation, which resulted in many silent moments that included staring into each other's eyes and playful kisses.

I knew where this was going. This could be the one night stand

I never experienced, and it could be perfect. He would be leaving the next day, so it was now or never. After dinner we walked hand in hand back to our hotel. We took a walk on the beach, and the seduction began; I was like putty in his hands. His awkward attempt in broken English to ask me up to his hotel room (to see more of his etchings) made me a bit nervous. He sensed this, and came up with the smoothest communication. "This would be a memory we could make together that would last a lifetime. When we have grandchildren we will think back and it will make us smile." It was funny how his English suddenly improved a bit.

Well, he almost had me, but there was still the issue of safe sex and using a condom. I was nervous and a bit embarrassed about bringing up the safe sex issue. The language barrier became frustrating after I used every possible word in English to describe a condom. He just kept looking at me, confused by what I was trying to say. Frustrated, I resorted to a game of charades. At last, he got it! He started laughing with a very sexy rasp as he said, "Oh, yes, a preservativo, *I have one!" Ding, ding, just like that, the light turned green.*

Let's just say that it was the best sex and not-so-great sex wrapped in one. The great sex part was in my head. I was with this very sexy Italian man for one night while I was vacationing on the Italian Riviera and he was an artist, for Christ's sake! The not-so-great sex part was that he had the smallest penis I ever met in my life; I could hardly feel him inside me. After we were done he begged me to stay the night, but I refused, using my waiting girlfriend as an excuse. It was sweet, sexy and perfect as I kissed him hard on the mouth and said good-bye as I walked out his door. He was right; I smile every time I think back to that night.

When I got home from my fantasy vacation, I had time to reflect on my experience. Life is a balancing act between playing it safe and taking chances. Looking back at my "Affair on the Italian Riviera," I wouldn't trade that night for anything in the world, but I struggled with my decision to take a chance. I was a pent-up sex kitten ready to pounce and prove my sexual prowess and desirability. It could have been ugly, but I responsibly did the best I could to protect myself by being sober and aware of everything that went on, practiced safe sex and, in the end, decided to let go and enjoy life. I was lucky, but the experience made me think about how I would handle myself now that I was home and ready to step out in the dating world. I promised myself that I would be cautious with my body to protect my health, but also to have a great time because life is short.

Lessons Learned

- Sex is an important part of marriage; friendship is critical, but you have to have both.

Now that you are armed with information on safety and how to maximize fun and success in the dating world, get ready to step out of your box and into a brave new world.

Chapter

8

Who Is Prince Charming?

PRINCE WHO!? That's the answer I got when I asked many women, "Who is Prince Charming?" They either responded with an eye roll or a telling cackle that confirmed he only existed in fairy tales. I almost sensed hostility from some women when this topic came up. They told me they felt like they had been misled about what it was going to be like as a married adult. It seemed many women bought into the idea, including yours truly, that the right man would be a guarantee for a "happily ever after." If he turned out to be the wrong man, our "power of love" could change him to be the prince we dreamed of. Those expectations fueled the beginning of our disappointment and frustration with the opposite sex. The idea that "love is all you need" to make a marriage work is a far cry from reality—many of us were just too naïve to know it.

I rephrased my question and asked: "Who is Prince Charming in the 'real world'?" Luckily, there was an immediate change in attitude and the conversation started to flow. Women were very open and candid with their insightful and sometimes funny answers of what he is and what he's most definitely not. Will the real Prince Charming please stand up?

One woman said she had dated a guy who fit what most women

207

would consider perfection. He came from money, was beautiful to look at and was also quite the dancer. They had mind-blowing sex and couldn't keep their hands off each other. After a few weeks of total euphoria, she had to break up with him because she realized that after achieving multiple orgasms, the only thing she wanted to do was get up and leave. After her hormones calmed down, her brain started functioning again, and she realized the guy was a "Fluffernutter." Her infatuation with his body and his "charm factor" lost their powerful blinding effects. She could see again and what lay next to her was a boring, conceited and incredibly miserable character who happened to have the most amazing abs. All he wanted to talk about was his money and his toys. He lacked true substance and an ability to carry on an intelligent conversation outside of his family's business and abdominal workout.

That experience helped her recognize her true "Prince Charming" when he came into her life; he's a guy she would have never considered in the past. She describes him as bald, very smart and a little soft around the middle. He's great with her kids, loves to laugh and turns her on with his smile. She laughs when she tells me he went out in the middle of the night to buy her extra-absorbent tampons and came back with a menstrual survival kit. It was a bag of chocolate Kisses to satisfy her menstrual monster as well as a tube of Clearasil to combat the monster zit that would likely arrive the next day. She said it's little things like that that make her love him more because he really gets who she is and makes an effort every day to make her feel special. She admits in the past she might have considered this man just another average toad in the dating pool. She was smart enough to look beyond the superficial package to find the whole package, a great friend and lover. When she gave him a chance and kissed him, he turned into her Prince Charming.

After listening to many women, it was clear that the qualifications of Prince Charming drastically change with age and experience. One eighty-year-old woman told me her Prince Charming turned out to be a gentleman who had been courting her for a little bit more than a year. It took her some time to open her eyes and see what an amazing man he was. Her vision became clear one night when he wrapped his sweater around her waist and walked behind her out of a restaurant after she accidentally wet her pants. The two of them shuffled slowly out of the restaurant together, and she was flushed from embarrassment. As they exited the building, she felt like she had hit an all-time low with her incontinence problem. It was then that he whispered in her ear how much he loved her. She said, "Go figure. After two unsuccessful marriages, my knight in shining armor turned out to be a fellow octogenarian who wore a hearing aid, needed glasses and suffered from occasional bouts of flatulence."

My mother can give many reasons why my dad is still her prince after all these years. He earned the title this year because he is so adaptive and sympathetic to her menopausal hot flashes. The only way she can sleep is to have the thermostat below 70 degrees. Rather than complaining, my dad puts on thermal pajamas in the middle of a Florida heat wave and crawls under the covers in their arctic bedroom. The two of them live happily ever after when waking from a restful night's hibernation at a blissfully cool 68 degrees. Not the romantic story I was expecting but it's just one example of the many different real-life reasons he is her Prince Charming. One of my mom's favorite things about my dad is his ability to make her laugh in difficult situations. Their long-term relationship works because of compromise, understanding, forgiveness and an ability to adapt to the many changes that occur over the course of a long marriage.

"Once Upon a Time" and "Happily Ever After"

Before long, I started to wonder where the whole perfect Prince Charming idea came from. After rereading some of my favorite childhood fairy tales, I did some research and found some of the original versions. I stumbled upon *Sleeping Beauty*, and there was nothing princely about the male character. In one of the original versions, it's not a kiss that awakens the fair maiden while she sleeps. Instead, the king or prince impregnates her during her slumber and then takes off. This young innocent maiden wakes months later when she gives birth to twins. Can you imagine her surprise?

This was quite the departure from Walt Disney's sanitized version that we all grew up with. These stories were told and rewritten so many times it's almost like the game telephone; after a while the original version gets so diluted the message is completely different. Walt Disney and many other men did a great job cleaning up the dark sides of these stories and indulged in much creative license to create their own fairy tales. That might explain why the male characters were portrayed as perfect little stud muffins who packed very large "swords" underneath their tights. If Disney was a woman, there would have been a much different spin on Prince Charming; in fact, he probably never would have made it to the storyboard because the idea for him was just too out there.

I wonder what really happened to Cinderella after the Prince bed her and wed her. What's really behind that knight in shining armor just might be an egotistical, controlling man who spends more time in the mirror than you do! Living with him on a daily basis might be nothing short of torture and regret.

I'm always suspicious when I see a married couple walk in who look like Ken and Barbie. The saying holds true: If it looks too good to be true, it probably is, because Barbie is usually miserable and Ken is a philandering fool. We put JFK and Jackie O on the Camelot pedestal until their perfect image of magically married with kids came tumbling down with a little help from Marilyn Monroe. All of this is so perfectly human and real, a far departure from the fairy tales we read as children.

The versions many of us grew up with launched our fantasies of being rescued and "once upon a time" and a "happily ever after." The idea of the perfect man created unreal expectations about the opposite sex. Many of us searched for the perfect guy and thought once he married us he would make us perfectly happy—after all it was his job. Unfortunately, once the honeymoon was over and reality set in, things were far from the perfection we expected. We started to feel disappointed, and the problems started.

I started to think about the idea of the perfect prince rescuing the beautiful princess—why did Disney think we all needed rescuing? On closer inspection of my favorite fairy tale, *Cinderella,* I see the characters from a different perspective as a grown woman. Prince Charming meets a girl at a fancy ball and falls head over heels in love with her. They dance and talk all night until she mysteriously disappears leaving behind a glass slipper. With this piece of footwear, the guy scours the countryside in search of the first woman whose foot fits into the shoe.

Right about now I'm thinking he can't be too bright because it's a stupid plan. Hundreds of women line up and try to convince the prince they are his lost love as they jam their huge feet into a tiny slipper that doesn't fit. The prince believes many of the imposters until others have to explain that the women are frauds. The prince seems a bit clueless and in need of rescuing from himself.

Let's examine this Cinderella character for a moment. Here is a strong young woman who has just lost her father. She is left in a home with an evil stepmother and two horrid sisters who torment her and treat her like a slave. Rather than become bitter from her circumstances, she remains true to her sweet, loving and adventurous nature. When she has an opportunity to attend a cool party and snag the most desirable bachelor in all the land, she goes for it. She has no problem going to the party by herself, and when she arrives she is no shrinking wall flower. She gets the hot guy's attention and dances all night. This does not sound like a woman who needs to be rescued.

Now if I was Cinderella, before I agreed to ride off in the sunset with this guy, I would need to do some serious thinking. I would be wondering if the prince had a foot fetish or if he was mentally challenged. Would I really want to spend the rest of my life with a guy who was searching for my foot? You would think that after spending an enchanted evening together he would be searching for my face or my voice. Just what am I really getting myself into here if I agree to hop onto his steed?

In the story Cinderella does ride off into the sunset with the prince. It always left me wondering what happened once they got to his parents' palace and he had his way with her. What does their "happily ever after" look like after the fairy dust is gone and they start living day in and day out with each other?

This immediately brings to mind the fractured fairy tale of Prince Charles the charming and Princess Diana. The whole world was mesmerized and glued to their TV sets the day the royal couple wed in holy matrimony. Diana was Cinderella brought to life. Everybody wanted to believe the fairy tale was possible, and for a few moments the world was filled with magic; Walt Disney would have been so proud. Unfortunately, the fairy tale was destroyed before it began and everyone mourned the loss of the dream. I don't think Walt would have been too surprised because after all he did live in the real world.

I wonder what fairy tales Diana read and what preconceived notions she had about love and marriage before and after her experience. She could have used a sequel to Cinderella that was written by a woman. After the magic dust wore off, Cinderella could have given her some tips on how to deal with the mother-in-law, the jealous maidens who were passed over, and the many royal obligations she had to undertake now that she was a princess.

Many women loved Diana because they could all relate to her struggle with her marriage and her low self-esteem. Like the ugly duckling, she was a beautiful swan hanging out with the wrong group, a bunch of compromised royal ducks. Her prince turned out to be a frog, and if she had recognized her own self-worth, she would have had the strength to reject an empty proposal. There were many regular guys out there who did not have the looks or title of Prince but would have appreciated everything and all that she was before it was too late.

Changing Expectations

The burdens and expectations some women place on men to sweep them off their feet and rescue them emotionally and financially are unrealistic, unfair and ridiculous. The idea of Prince Charming falls short not because he falls off of his great white horse, but because he never climbed on to begin with and probably never wanted to. I wonder if Prince Charles would rather have been born a regular guy without having to live up to all of the royal expectations.

Relationships are not about male and female roles and responsibilities. It's about two people coming together and working in a partnership toward their unique happily-ever-after. For success, both partners need to consider each other as equals. There should be a natural flow of give and take where each partner feels like they are getting what they need from the relationship. As a woman, I can't imagine wanting to put a man on a pedestal and slave away to take care of his every desire. Any man who would even want to attempt this could use some serious psychotherapy or would be doing so with some major strings attached.

One of my favorite lines in a movie is from *Pretty Woman* with Julia Roberts and Richard Gere. In one scene he climbs up a fire escape to proclaim his love for her. He kisses her and asks, "What happens now that the prince rescues the princess?" She smiles at him and without hesitation replies, "She rescues him right back." Now that's the beginning of the modern day fairy tale. What lies ahead for them will no doubt have its ups and downs, but hopefully they will work hard as partners as they pave their way to enjoying their journey in life together. Prince Charming can exist in the real world, but his qualities and traits would be quite different from our fairy tales.

I have seen some of Disney's latest fairy tales with my children. Not only are these stories amazing, the message is totally different. The female characters are about strong women who can stand on their own, and their mantra is all about girl power. Some of the female characters are saying, "Yes, I love you and want to marry you but first I want to get my medical degree." On top of that the prince characters are not just pretty faces with huge bank accounts and one-track minds. Some of them are worldly, interesting, open-minded and excellent listeners. Others are big fat ogres with great big hearts who offer a great capacity for friendship and love. They are all far from perfect but they are princes in their own right. It just depends on the perspective and desires of the woman looking to find her match.

These stories are now evolving more into what I like to call a "reality tale." The characters are far from perfect, and their relationships have flaws that they learn to work out together. These stories are great because there is a clear message that each character is responsible for his or her own happiness before a relationship can work. Some of these lessons could have helped our generation get more realistic about relationships and the expectations men and women have of each other and themselves.

If we are more realistic and have a better idea of who we are, there still is a good chance to find a happily ever after, it's just a different picture that needs a new frame.

Creating Your Own "Reality Tale"

There are many things you learn as you work your way through divorce. You definitely get to know yourself better and have more of an education about relationships. Your experience helps you understand what you need in your new life and what you want to avoid in the future. The biggest lesson is that no man is going to rescue you from your ivory tower and deliver you a happily ever after. Even if he promises to and his intentions are good, he will ultimately fail because nobody can rescue you except yourself. The reality and the journey to your unique happily ever after require a lot of effort on your part with an open heart and open mind.

To help me get through some of my worst divorce moments, I escaped into my daydreams. I was the heroine in my own "reality tale" that was yet to play itself out. I had many different scenarios of what I wanted to do and the type of guy I wanted to meet down the road. I was confident I would find my happiness again with or without a man. I was taking care of myself and refused to let the negative energy get the best of me—although I definitely had my moments.

By the time I came out of my ordeal, I was doing great. I never felt better about myself and my happiness seemed to be contagious. I was attracting wonderful things and people into my life. I've learned that part of the "reality tale" is learning to celebrate and appreciate the little things along the way rather than waiting for some man to come in and change your life. Living through something so difficult gives you the gift to recognize many wonderful things in life that others take for granted or just fail to see. Divorce gives you the common sense to know when you have it good. I can say I have a deeper sense of happiness; when something good comes into my life I enjoy it more and savor it until all the juice is squeezed out of it.

I interviewed a woman I knew who had a happy marriage, and we talked about what made her marriage work. Her formula was a great friendship because she happened to marry the right guy. They both understood that they needed to work at the relationship, which helped them to grow up together through the years. The next day after our lunch she called me to thank me. I was surprised because she was the one doing me the favor by letting me interview her. She explained that I was her wake-up call to remember what a great marriage and life she had with her husband. She said after our chat she realized just how many wonderful things she took for granted. She said she had it good for so long, she stopped imagining what it was like for it to be bad. She was going to make a new habit of focusing more on the positives in her life rather than let the silly negatives suck out all of her energy.

Prince Charming Is . . .

Who is your Prince Charming now that you've been through the ringer and know reality from fiction? When I asked never-married young women about Prince Charming qualities, they looked starry eyed. After pondering the question, they came back with answers that were generalities, such as good-looking, athletic and makes a good living.

In contrast, women of divorce have a knowing look in their eyes. They answer without hesitation and zero in on one particular quality they didn't get in their marriage, which is now a non-negotiable item in their next mate. Their make or break quality came from their experience of divorce, which gave them a better understanding of who they were, what they needed in a relationship and what they were not going to tolerate. Outside of a few angry women who chanted, "First I married for love, this time I'm marrying for money," I got some good answers of what qualities in a mate can make a solid relationship. The answers were much different from the ideal man many of us had in our heads when we were younger.

Here is one woman's story of finding an imposter who she originally thought was Prince Charming. She said the outside package was great, but in real life it was more trouble than it was worth, and he turned out to be a real toad on the inside. She learned from her experience, which helped her to create her happy new beginning by opening her eyes to her real prince.

*a*lice—42 years old

I was married to a jock stud muffin for over fifteen years. Women would always swoon over him and make comments to me about how handsome he was. Instead of taking it as a compliment or even a threat, all I could react with in my head was, "Yeah right, you can have him." He really did look like Prince Charming from the outside. The problem was that he treated me horribly; all I could see was ugliness from the inside out.

I lived the life of luxury and was the object of many women's jealousy. If they only knew how unloved and miserable I was, they would probably realize what a catch their own husbands were. My spouse was a great package on the outside but was empty and void on the inside. For years I suffered from his neglect and emotional abuse. People who got to know him well would call him an empty suit.

I was lonely during my marriage and found myself attracted to many different men I would fantasize about. I found myself attracted to what I would have called in the past nerdy looking guys who were soft spoken and very intelligent. I would talk to them and felt like I could melt in their words because they were sincere, sweet-hearted men. I remember having a visceral response being around some of them because I just wanted them to hold me, love me and talk to me like I was someone who mattered.

I eventually divorced and five years later married the most wonderful man. My friends from college met him the day of our wedding, and they were surprised by his average looks. He has thinning hair, glasses and a voice that makes my knees shake in a good way. My true love looks like nothing I imagined, but he is my true Prince Charming. His personality and qualities turn me on, and I couldn't be any more in love with this kind, intellectually stimulating, sweet, sexy man. He also turned out to be a great dad, makes the bed in the morning and helps around the house, which are things I never realized were so important to have in a marriage. He's the guy who kept me company all night when I was hunched over the toilet with the stomach flu. I think I'm turned on to him more over time because of all of the wonderful things he is and does for me and the kids. By the way, he is now completely bald—and I love it!

Unfortunately, I saw my old marriage play out with one of my best friends from college. She has been locked in miserable matrimony with her Adonis husband for the last twelve years. When I ask her why she didn't leave and escape the emotional abuse and infidelity she said, "I would hate to lose such a good-looking man." She admitted to me that it made her feel good that the outside world looked at her with appraising eyes because she was able to land such a good-looking guy.

Her self-esteem was wrapped around her husband's looks; it didn't matter that he treated her like a doormat behind their closed doors because to the outside world they were the pretty couple. She couldn't bring herself to leave him. It was no surprise *when her husband left her for another woman. Now my friend is really struggling to pick herself up and start again. She tells me how smart I was to leave my first marriage and find a real man. By the way, I ran into my ex a few weeks back, and he's losing his hair and getting fat.*

Lessons Learned

- Looks fade so you'd better like the person you're with because the superficial package alone is just not worth the aggravation. You can't grow old with a pretty face and tight abs.
- Personality, compatibility and attraction are the magical ingredients.

Now, will more of the real Prince Charming types please stand up? Here is a group of women who have some very specific ideas of who their prince is. Nothing was mentioned about appearance, but they all agreed that, along with these great traits and qualities, there most definitely still had to be attractive.

Kelly—37 years old

A Strong Man

I want a hybrid of a man's man and a gentleman's gentleman who knows how to treat and respect the woman in his life. I'm thinking about the burly Marlboro man with a little tweaking. When we walk into a restaurant filled with other attractive women, he's the guy who pulls the chair out for me and makes me feel like I'm the only one worth looking at.

I'm done with the metrosexual type who has more grooming products for his hair than I do. You know what I'm talking about, he's the guy who spends too much time in front of the mirror and shaves more body parts than any woman possibly could. I want my guy to smell like a man, look like a man yet still know how to turn up the heat for some romance.

My strong man has traditional values and is confident and worthy of my respect in his business and personal life. When I'm with him I feel safe and well protected; I know he can take care of me even though I can take care of myself. He's a guy I can learn from and become a better person just by being in his company.

Jennifer—31 years old

An Honest Man

I remember watching an interview with the actress Halle Berry. She was asked to choose the one thing she needed to have in a relationship with a man. I knew what her answer was before she opened her mouth; it was complete and absolute honesty. I could totally relate to this woman because, like her, I was married to a man I thought I knew but who was really a complete stranger. He turned out to be a pathological liar who was dishonest in his work and led a double life with another woman. My experience was so devastating because I realized with some people you can never tell what is truly in their heart. I want a guy I can look at and know for sure that he is true blue, what you see is truly what you get.

Susan—38 years old

A Forgiving Man

I was in a marriage with a man who would never truly forgive me for any of the arguments and disagreements we had. Our relationship could never start with a clean slate because he kept score of every negative interaction we had. We might have had great makeup sex, but he always kept things in the back of his mind to throw back in my face. His lack of forgiveness and an inability to truly move on and start fresh infected our relationship. He grew less loving and less kind to me through the years, and he eventually festered in disgust for me.

My Prince Charming is a guy who understands I'm not perfect. He accepts me for who I am and totally forgives and knows how to move forward and start again with a clean slate. Even when I am at my worst, he is able to look at me in a way that tells me, yeah, you're being a shit now but I still love you. He understands that couples will have issues, and when you work out some of the kinks, you can become stronger and more connected to one another.

Nadine—41 years old

A Man Who Can Make Me Laugh

I'm a very serious person, and I made the mistake of marrying someone who is even more intense than I am. All of our arguments and disagreements became debates that escalated out of control. From my experience I realized I'm the type of person who needs a man who can make me laugh to help balance my intensity and seriousness. My dream man is somebody who knows how to break the tension by doing something funny when *things get too heated. I would love a man who knows that life is too short to live without laughter and can teach me how to be silly.*

Roxanne—33 years old

A Friend

I had to learn the hard way that a relationship is more than just great sex because friendship is what really makes it work. My ex-husband seemed to have the capacity to be a great friend to men but didn't really like or respect women. He was the ultimate guy's guy. The phone would never stop ringing for him because he was like the camp counselor planning wonderful activities with "the guys."

I want a man who enjoys the company of a woman outside of the bedroom and the kitchen. He will treat me like an equal friend and show me kindness and respect. We share responsibilities and cross over the male/female roles of who cooks and takes out the garbage depending on who's around to do it. We take care of each other equally in ways that are constantly changing. There is a good balance of give and take with a daily effort not to take the other for granted, like not putting down the toilet seat.

Beth—40 years old

A Communicator

I understand that "men are from Mars and women are from Venus." I also understand that if I wanted a man to be able to talk to me like my girlfriends, I should probably change my sexual preference and become a lesbian. However, I need to know I can have a back-and-forth dialogue with a man when issues come up so we can constructively work them out. I shouldn't feel that a conversation between us is like going to the dentist to get teeth pulled.

I won't stay in another relationship where every discussion starts with me talking in a calm and warm manner only to be met with a blank look and no comment. I need to know that when I express myself there will be someone on the other end who can do more than just grunt or roll his eyes.

My girlfriend told me about a discussion she just had with her boyfriend that gave me hope. She expressed her feelings about something that was bothering her, and he listened without replying. When she asked why he looked like he was in pain, he honestly said that he wasn't used to talking about issues. He admitted that he had a problem because even though she had a valid point and expressed her feelings without attacking him, he still felt like a scolded school boy. He said he needed to grow up because he learned from his last relationship why couples need to address issues. He asked her to be patient with him as he tried to open up and actually talk about things.

I couldn't believe it, a guy who admits he is a bad communicator who wants to work at it and understands how important it is. I asked if he had a brother.

Sandy—55 years old

A Man Who Will Give Me My Space

I have been single for the last twenty years, and I have become quite comfortable in my own skin and my lifestyle. I don't want to get married again and don't even feel comfortable living with somebody. I would like a man who can deal with my independence but understands my desire for intimacy, intellectual stimulation and friendship.

Tania—43 years old

I grew up as an only child in a home where my dad spoiled my mom and me with love and attention. We were his life, and he treated us like royalty, we always had whatever we needed and wanted. On Friday nights he would come home after work with a beautiful bouquet of red roses for my mom and a box of candy for me. I have memories of my mom and dad dancing in the living room to Frank Sinatra. My childhood was a fairy tale; I just didn't know it at the time because to me it was just a normal life.

When I started dating, I wanted to find somebody "just like Daddy." In my mind the right boy would want to take care of my every need and shower me with gifts and compliments. The beginnings of my courtships were wonderful; there were lots of flowers, love letters and attention. Unfortunately, all of my relationships were short-lived. They ended one of two ways; I got bored with the guy, or the guy got disgusted with me because they said I was too high maintenance and way too spoiled. I was shocked to hear their description of me, especially when I felt like I was just like my mother, and my dad thought she was perfect.

My mother was a homemaker whose life revolved around taking care of us, shopping and lunching with her friends. She was always quiet and shy but seemed relatively happy. It wasn't until I grew older that I sensed she was restless and bored with her life. One day my dad got into a car accident and had to be hospitalized for a few months; luckily he made a full recovery. It was a huge strain, especially for my mother. Right before my eyes she became unglued after putting up a good front for my father. It was the first time in her life she had to take care of things and herself without my dad. The woman could barely function; she had no idea how to balance a checkbook, pay the bills or be alone.

Every night she camped out in the hospital and only went home to shower and have an occasional meal.

What became clear to me during this difficult time was how much my parents loved each other. What surprised me was how incapable my mother was without my father. Here was a grown woman who was still a scared little girl who needed someone to take care of her on a daily basis. I started to think that the description sounded a lot like me. She was completely dependent and totally lost without him.

One day we talked about things and she admitted to having been unhappy for a long time. She said it wasn't about my dad so much as it was about her lack of purpose and low self-esteem. She admitted that in the beginning of their marriage, being put up on a pedestal by Dad felt great. However, over the years his love and doting became too much of a crutch for her to lean on. She started feeling like she was living in a prison, isolated from the rest of the real world. That was the moment I realized my parents were real people. The illusion of the fairy tale was gone when I learned my parents had real issues and a real marriage with problems that needed to be worked out. Their fairy tale was showing signs of reality, and things were about to get interesting.

A few months after my father made a complete recovery, our house was suddenly filled with constant bickering between my parents. It was a drastic departure from the peaceful, loving relationship I witnessed growing up. I got my mother alone and asked her what was happening. She said that she wanted to focus on her life for a change and start doing things that made her happy. She was sick of not speaking her mind all of these years and letting Dad make all of the decisions. She explained that he was having a hard time dealing with the fact that suddenly she had a mouth and an opinion on everything. Their arguing was nonstop and they are still going at it to this day.

The thought of trying to find a husband "just like Daddy" was starting to sound a bit perverse and not in my best interest. In the end, I married a guy completely different from my dad. His attitude toward our relationship and marriage was that we were both full and equal partners. I fell in love with him because he treated me like an adult, not a little child who needed to be taken care of. His attitude helped me grow up and take responsibility for myself. I found a great career and enjoy my work, my life and my family. My husband is the icing on top of a cake I made by myself. He makes everything sweeter, but I'm what makes my life work. I was able to learn how to take care of myself but still share a life with a man where we take care of each other.

I found my Prince Charming and he turned out to be the antithesis of my dad. I was smart enough to choose a man who would help me to reach my potential as a person so we could grow up together as a couple. I can't tell you that I don't miss the lavish attention and unconditional love I got from my dad, but marrying someone just for that would have been a mistake. I have a good, solid marriage and we are well matched for each other. My husband is the type of guy who helps push me out of the nest so I can learn to fly on my own and become the person I wanted to be. Together we are raising a beautiful, confident girl. She will have no problem taking care of herself as she learns to stand on her own two feet. I feel like she has a realistic picture of marriage and the world around her. She knows that a modern day "happily ever after" starts with finding it in herself first.

Side Notes

Many men who have been divorced can actually be quite the catch. Sure, they come with baggage, but so do you. After interviewing many men, they said they learned from their mistakes and felt they make a much better mate than they did in the past. A few have even agreed that what most women want is really not so much to ask for or that hard to deliver. They agreed that it required making a conscious effort not to get lazy or take a woman for granted. By paying attention to the little things, and maintaining trust and friendship, they saw their new relationships thrive. They felt that their efforts were well worth it because they would get so much more back in return. On the other hand, there are some male divorce-rejects out there just waiting to torture another female. Inspect all potential candidates carefully for unsavory traits and characteristics.

A good way to know if he's your prince is if he has seen you at your worst and still loves you, even though he might not like you at the moment. I'm not talking about a bad hair day where you are sleep deprived and have no makeup on to cover up that PMS zit you are now sporting for a third eye. Nope, that stuff is way too basic. I'm talking about the evil side of you who's a witch's potion of bitterness, depression, biting irritability with a shot of Olympic level bitchiness. The "you" that nobody should be subjected to, not even a dog. Yup, that's the one I'm talking about. If he's seen that you and he can handle it without calling 911, he just might be a keeper.

Who Is the Post-Divorce Princess Charming?

Now that we got that whole Prince Charming thing out of the way, it's time to forget about him and focus on something more important— YOU! Start focusing on what a fabulous package you can be as you climb out of divorce with a new perspective and lease on life. Living through divorce changes you to the core and in the most positive ways—if you make that choice. I interviewed many women of divorce who successfully moved on with their lives to experience more happiness and peace of mind than they ever have before. Some of them are in a committed relationship, while others are enjoying the benefits of being single.

My first question in my interviews was, "What lessons have you learned from divorce that make you a great woman?"

Donna—46 years old

I once heard someone say that you learn more from the things that go wrong in your life than the things that go right. I have certainly had my share of things going wrong. As a result, I've had great opportunities to learn, which has helped me to be the best person I can be. The most important thing is a healthy self-esteem, which I can't say enough about. Next was a realization that when it comes to men and women in relationships, there will never be perfection. It's the unique imperfections that make people interesting and attractive.

I think that what makes me a great woman is that I'm finally comfortable in my own skin, warts and all. I now choose to be around people who build me up and accept all that I am. My current boyfriend is a guy who pursued me for months until I accepted the first date. It's been over a year and if you ask him what he likes most about me, his answer would be that I'm wonderfully quirky. My ex-husband used to hate that about me, and I would let his dislike tear me down. I finally realized the power of making a choice to be around people who like and accept who I am.

Ann—45 years old

In my first marriage I had unrealistic expectations about marriage and expected my spouse to be everything to me, including a mind reader. I wanted him to do things for me the way I wanted him to do them; it wasn't enough that he made the effort to try and make me happy. We went for couples counseling, but the good news is that we eventually divorced. I did walk away with a great lesson on expectations.

Here is an example of the new me in my new relationship with my boyfriend. One night I was watching TV in the den and my boyfriend was in the kitchen. I asked him if he could get me some ice cream. Five minutes later he hands me a glob of ice cream in a plastic cup with an enormous spoon. I smiled and thanked him even though what I had in mind was something totally different. I wanted a perfect round scoop of ice cream in my petite glass dessert bowl drizzled with chocolate syrup with a dessert spoon and a napkin.

The old me would have complained that what he gave me wasn't what I had in mind. I probably would have droned on and said if he really loved me he would know what I want and how I wanted it. Now that I can step away from myself I realize just how absurd that is—nobody is a mind reader and nobody is going to do it exactly my way. In the end, I asked for ice cream and I got my ice cream and that is all that matters. I have learned to smile and say thank you when I get what I want. That simple example has carried over to many aspects of my new relationship and perspective.

I realized that men are never going to be perfect, and if they were perfect like us (hah hah), it would be too predictable and boring. I think women sometimes sabotage a good thing because their expectations are so high and so specific, they lose the big picture. Similar to the old me, some women don't see what they are getting because they put too much focus on what they aren't getting. I learned that a man can't give me everything, but if he *gives me those things that are really important to me then he is my Prince Charming.*

Angela—39 years old

What makes me a great woman is that I'm no longer afraid of my life. Divorce has taught me that there are so many things I have no control over and never will. Before my divorce I felt like there were times I was running scared. I was a control freak and got caught up in the minutia of my life. I was very rigid, followed all the rules and was uncomfortable in my skin if I didn't have everything just so. Living through a divorce has helped me let go of a lot of my fear and control issues. As a result, I feel like my spirit has been liberated. For the first time in a long time I can breathe, exhale and enjoy my life.

I started dating this great guy and for the first time I went into it with no expectations about the future and an attitude to just enjoy the moment. On our second date, he asked me to hop on the back of his motorcycle and take a ride through town. The first thing that came into my head was that there was no way I could do that, my dad made me promise I would never ride a motorcycle. Five seconds later I thought to myself, Snap out of it, you're not a kid anymore; it's time to stop being so scared of everything. I decided to have an adventure and live for that moment so off we went, with a helmet on my head for safety and a promise he would keep the speed down.

What a great experience—I loved the way it felt and the sense of freedom I had. I think the most exhilarating part was that I did something far out of my little controlled zone and survived it with a big smile on my face. It was a turning point in my life, and it gave me a feeling of breaking free from the old and starting a new life of freedom, adventure and endless possibilities.

I have also discovered that riding behind a guy on a motor-cycle is a great experience for all of the senses. I finally understood what Lauren Hutton meant when she said, "If I can't have a man underneath me, I'd like to be on top of a motorcycle." It's like sitting on the biggest vibrator in the world. Picture your legs straddled around a guy's middle from behind as you hold on for dear life. You move in unison with him while on top of a machine that is warm and goes hummmm. It's an adrenaline rush in so many ways and so many unexpected places. It really is the closest thing to sex I ever experienced. I think my boyfriend knew exactly what he was doing when he got me on that bike.

As far as the guy, we are enjoying each other's company and there is no pressure from either side. Whether "he's the one" doesn't matter; he is the one for this moment and time. I am happy to say that I have turned into someone I don't recognize at times, and I like what I see and how I feel, especially when I'm on that bike!

Princess Charming Is . . .

I asked one woman who she has become after her divorce. She looked at me without hesitation and said "'Princess Charming,' and some guy would be damn lucky to win my heart." I started asking women what qualities make up a Princess Charming type. They said after the experience of divorce, she is a woman who:

- Takes a good hard look at her part in the demise of her old relationship and accepts personal responsibility. She looks at divorce as a challenge and an opportunity to learn and evolve as a person and sees her life as a new chapter that will be filled with adventure. She is willing to step out of her box and take some chances, and when she feels scared and shy about going out on her own, she pushes herself outside of her comfort zone anyway. When she needs that extra shove out the door, she remembers that even Cinderella had the courage to go to the party by herself.

- Has a better understanding of who she is and what she needs in life and from a mate in a relationship. She is not affected by expectations from the outside world. She knows herself well and can identify a potential mate who fills her needs, even if it's a questionable choice to family and friends. She has come "into her own" and lives as her true, authentic self.

- Is not looking for a fairy tale but a reality tale where two people who love each other learn to be perfectly human and happy together. She does her best to avoid old destructive behavior, and if she slips, she forgives herself and quickly changes negative action into something positive. She is more realistic about what a relationship is and what it requires. Before jumping into another marriage, she asks herself whether she is actually cut out for that kind of commitment again. She is honest with herself and her partner and is careful with her choice of words, trying not to use them as weapons.

- Forgives herself and her ex so she can move forward in her life without carrying that baggage. This is especially critical if children are involved. She will find a way to make a co-parenting relationship work peacefully. This will have a positive impact on the children and avoid poisoning future relationships as she starts her new life.

- Really likes and respects who she is and is comfortable on her own. She makes a daily effort to be good to herself and makes having fun a priority. She does not need to search for a man to fill a void. She is financially and emotionally healthy and does not need somebody to take care of her. She would like to find someone to share the journey of life together on equal footing but knows that if it doesn't happen she can be happy on her own.

- Has become harder and softer. Harder in the sense of being strong enough to handle almost any challenge or difficulty that comes her way. Her mantra is, "If I survived that, I can survive anything." However, her journey through divorce has also left her a much softer and gentler soul. When dealing with someone who is being unreasonable or difficult, she reminds herself that there probably is a reason for their behavior; instead of being reactive, she offers kindness and compassion.

The Male Wish List

Out of curiosity, I asked men what they really wanted from women and what they looked for in a long-term mate. After some tongue and cheek comments from married and single male friends, like "She needs to have really good suction," I got down to some serious interviewing.

There is no doubt that there is a percentage of the male population out there who should have warning signs stamped on their foreheads. Their morals, values and ideas of relationships could wreak havoc on some unsuspecting women. In all fairness, I have to admit I met a few female counterparts with similar qualities that could be just as dangerous to the trusting, well-intentioned male.

The good news is that, as a majority, I met some wonderful men with good hearts and intentions. Once I got to know them through the interviews, I realized just how many potential diamonds in the rough are really out there. I became relieved and even more hopeful when I learned men really do want a lot of the same things woman want in a long-term committed relationship. They were able to narrow their wish list without much trouble. Their responses to what they want in a woman were simple and basic, but I pressed for more details and specifications. It was a bit like pulling teeth in the beginning, but a lot of men did open up and here is what they had to say:

GOOD LOOKS—I'm not talking "super model" looks, but she has to know how to take care of herself. I want to see that a woman takes pride in her appearance. If a woman just lets herself go and doesn't care about what she looks like, it makes me think she has some mental issues. She doesn't have to be perfect or drop-dead gorgeous, but her package has to work for me. The effort she puts into keeping her body fit and pulling it all together says a lot about her. Looking good has a big impact on confidence, and a woman with confidence is a big turn-on.

SEX—I want sex, my body needs sex, I must have sex. A long-term relationship can't revolve around it, but I want it to be fun and uninhibited. I think the main element of great sex is great communication. I want her to tell me what she likes, and I need to feel comfortable enough to express my desires as well. I want a woman who is not uncomfortable with her body regardless of her size.

FRIENDSHIP—Good looks and good sex are important, but it means nothing long term if you're not the best of friends. Having a good friendship is probably the most important quality to maintaining a healthy, long-term relationship. I want to come home and talk about my day to someone who is a great listener and really wants to hear what I have to say. I also want to come home to someone who is interesting and has her own thing going on as well. I don't want to feel like her world revolves around mine; I want us to be able to learn from each other. I want to know I can come to her and be able to talk with her about anything and everything.

Love and Marriage

When two people are under the influence of the most violent, most insane, most delusive, and most transient of passions, they are required to swear that they will remain in that excited, abnormal, and exhausting condition continuously until death do them part.

—George Bernard Shaw

I just attended the wedding of a young girl I used to babysit for. As I sat in my chair fresh off the divorce experience, I watched these two innocent people take their marriage vows for the first time. My immediate thought was, *If they only knew what they were getting themselves into.* After a few minutes of looking at them gaze into each other's eyes, my feelings gave way to hope and the possibility that they really could create their happily ever after together. I was relieved that I hadn't become completely jaded from my divorce experience; I still believe you can be happily married and create your own "reality tale." My experience in my marriage and divorce has given me valuable lessons to create healthier relationships in the future. I realized that getting to my happily ever after is a much different journey than I originally thought.

Doris—72 years old

A good marriage starts with a strong foundation. The cement must be poured with the right amount of friendship, attraction and respect to avoid any major cracks. Having respect for one another is so important, and I just don't see enough of that in today's young people.

I think the first step is being smart enough to pick the right fellow. Your expectations should certainly be high but at the same time realistic. No man is ever going to be able to give you everything you need and want. It's up to you to fill in your voids with other people and activities that make you feel whole and happy. As a woman, expect to put 110 percent effort into the relationship. If your spouse puts in at least 75 to 80 percent you are doing just fine.

Once you have found the right man, you have to form a strong partnership that nothing and nobody can break apart. Even when you get angry at each other and face tough times, you have to keep in mind that you are on the same team no matter what. Marriage will be more work and compromise than you ever imagined, and there will always be challenging ups and downs. However, the joy you get from sharing your life with someone special is worth all the blood, sweat and tears.

We all have a childhood dream that when there is love, everything goes like silk, but the reality is that marriage requires a lot of compromise.

—Raquel Welch

Many couples—where one or both partners were previously divorced—said that it took them one practice marriage to figure it out and get it right the next time around. Getting it right required three major things. First is getting to know yourself well enough to know what you want in a mate so you can make a better choice. Second is being strong enough to stand on your own but making a choice to stand together without getting lost. The next part involves being conscious about not repeating destructive behavior that contributed to problems in prior relationships, specifically taking the other for granted.

Marriage is not a ritual or an end. It is a long, intricate, intimate dance together and nothing matters more than your own sense of balance and your choice of partner.

—Amy Bloom

Try to find a mate that will bring out your better qualities. When your "stuff" occasionally rears its ugly head, consider it a great quality if your partner can help you to take it down a notch. For instance, if I was acting irrationally in my old marriage, it would set my spouse off and we would have a fight that would only escalate. In my new relationship, my boyfriend has this calm way that can gently nudge me to a place where I realize how ridiculous I'm being, and many times it ends in laughter.

In the end, you and no one else are responsible for your actions, reactions, attitudes and perceptions. You will be the one to create the world in which you live. A person can bring out the worst in you or help you to become a better person, but ultimately the responsibility lies within you to be the best person you can be.

Riding Off into the Sunset . . . Again?

In the beginning, many women come out of divorce feeling very cynical about relationships. It was shocking to hear the statistic that says close to 70 percent of the divorced population will remarry within three years of their divorce. When the question if I would ever marry again first came up, I cringed at the possibility. I was used to functioning as a single person in my marriage so I found my new title as Ms. to be a smooth transition and I liked it. I have a very busy calendar with my single and married friends, who always make me comfortable in social settings. I don't feel the stigma of not being married; I have too much fun feeling free and at peace with myself.

I remember having lunch with a man who had been divorced for many years. He felt the same way I did. He found humor when his friends asked him when he was going to settle down and marry again. He imagined a cartoon balloon over their heads that said, "We are sick of you having so much fun. We want you to be like us, married and miserable."

Having been through the experience of divorce makes you redefine marriage and how you look at relationships in the real world. Your expectations of what you want in a man are still high but more realistic. You also have a better idea of what it takes to make a relationship work.

Statistics show most people will take another chance at marriage or engage in some long-term relationship. My experience has taught me that a committed relationship, married or not, has to have more than just love involved. I fell in love with the wrong man and lived for over ten years in a dysfunctional marriage that was filled with tension and frustration for both of us. Eventually it fell apart because our love and attraction were not enough to hold us together.

I still believe in romance, but love at first sight really does need a second and third look before jumping back in. There are many things to consider when looking at a long-term relationship with a man, especially if you live together or marry. You probably had stars in your eyes the first time you married and didn't have a clue about what you were getting yourself into. Now that you know better, when it comes to living with someone day in and day out, love is a critical component but there are also some other very important considerations.

Ask yourself and each other: How well do you get along outside of the bedroom? Is sex just one of many great activities you enjoy together, like playing tennis or hanging out over dinner with a glass of wine and talking to each other? Are you a neatnik and is he a slob? Do you share common interests? If he's a big partier and likes to drink and you can't stand the taste of alcohol and what it does to your body, you might run into problems. How well do you fight and resolve issues? How long will you stay mad at each other even after apologies? Do you have the same values and dreams? What are your expectations of each other? If children are involved, are you willing to take on that responsibility, and do you share similar parenting beliefs? Is there a crazy ex-wife involved? What does the money situation look like, and are you able to talk about those responsibilities? Can you agree on lifestyle expenditures and how you will manage your money?

I'm not trying to make it sound like a business deal because it's not. However, now more than ever you realize the nuts and bolts of what makes a partnership work or not work. Being single for a time makes you independent; the trick is can you maintain that feeling of self when you get involved with a new partner? The list can go on and on, but this careful evaluation is critical. You don't want to go into another marriage with your eyes only half opened so they can bug out later in your next divorce.

Rethinking Your Reality Tale

Some of you will have a much different opinion and idea of how your next few chapters in life will look. You may make a choice to ride off into the sunset as a single person and enjoy your freedom and life a la carte.

If you want to sacrifice the admiration of many men for the criticism of one, go ahead, get married.

—Katharine Hepburn

Hepburn's quote definitely has a bit of bite to it. Your wounds might need some extra time to heal before you even consider getting into another serious relationship. Marrying again might not even be a consideration because it holds no interest for you. I found that many women who are older are content to stay single and enjoy their freedom to do what they want and not have to worry about taking care of someone else.

To love oneself is the beginning
of a lifelong romance.

—Oscar Wilde

Many women I talked to seem to fall into two categories: the Antimarriage Woman and the I Can't Wait to Get Married Again Woman. The Antimarriage Woman refuses to date for quite some time, and when she eventually ventures out, she is skeptical and has her radar on full alert for any red flags. She is slow to trust, but her desire and need for sex pushes her to look for a committed relationship without wanting a certificate of marriage to bind her.

In fact, many more people are choosing not to marry again because they don't have to. Our society has changed, and so have our definitions of what makes up a family. It's no longer just the people we marry or are connected to by birth. Today, family is made up of people we choose to share the times of our life with.

Women no longer have to marry to have children, and they can support themselves. There is much less pressure financially and socially to run off and marry again. Women who might consider marriage down the road are content to take more time to make sure the man they are with is truly marriage material before taking another leap of faith. This is true especially if they already have children and don't hear the ticking of their biological clock.

Then there are other women who have a burning desire to hunt down a new man and get married as soon as possible. Many of them haven't worked through their own issues. They marry the first guy who comes along and makes them feel good. It's a total rebound phenomenon that can happen when the divorce papers are still hot off the press. A rebound marriage can result from financial pressure, fear of being alone, the desire to procreate or just pure desperation. These marriages are usually doomed for failure because some women catapult themselves from the frying pan back into the fire, and their quick fix winds up being a disaster.

As I mentioned, the statistics show that most of you will remarry, even if the thought of it makes you want to break out in hives at the moment. Time will pass and the bitterness of what you went through will turn to sweetness as you start to enjoy your new life and the new people you meet.

If and when you make a choice to commit to someone, in a sense you are riding off into the sunset again hoping for the best. It's a bit of a risk to give your heart away and try again, but if you listen to your head and do the work on yourself, your chances of succeeding in your next relationship will be much greater.

Marriage is the triumph of imagination over intelligence. Second marriage is the triumph of hope over experience.

—Oscar Wilde

You can use the experience of your divorce to your advantage or disadvantage. Your happily ever after depends on learning from your failed relationship as you work on creating new healthier ones. Don't let your bad experience with marriage leave you bitter and untrusting because then you really do lose. If you choose not to learn from your experience, you will likely repeat your past with the same type of guy and the same mistakes. You are at a crossroads when you find a new man you are about to get serious with. First, evaluate your choice and consider the questions discussed earlier to make sure he really could be the right guy. If he is worth going to the next level, be conscious of not making the same mistakes and be open.

Part of healing and letting go will be your ability to forgive, and once again be able to love like you've never lost. You can do it. You are an emotional survivor who is stronger from the experience; you are nurturing your heart and soul, which makes you more capable of love and compassion. You are a princess warrior waiting for your next adventure . . .

A Final Note

I can't believe I'm writing the end of this book; it has been a friend to me, and I hope it's been the same for you. I'm finding it hard to let go of my time typing away at the keyboard as I put down my thoughts and the words of many women's stories and lessons. It's been three years of soul searching and interviewing strangers and friends. They trusted me enough to open up their lives for the sake of helping others heal who are on a similar path. I am forever grateful for their generosity of heart and soul. Their wisdom and perspective have been great gifts to help others navigate the challenging journey of divorce and beyond.

It can start out as surviving one awful day at a time where you feel like you can barely catch your breath. Your emotions are raw, and there will be days you might feel like you are on the verge of a nervous breakdown. I promise that those intense, uncomfortable feelings won't last forever and one day your divorce won't be an all-consuming thought.

Life will move on and, although it may seem hard to believe now, you will be happy again. You will come to realize that your divorce has given you a chance at a new beginning. You are a wiser, transformed woman who has experienced the sweet and sour of relationships. This makes you better equipped to know when you come upon something that is truly great in yourself and others. You are once again free to find your reality tale, but this time you are more knowledgeable to help you find your unique happily ever after.

I am still hopeful about love and marriage. What touches me the most and reveals the power of true love is when I see an elderly couple walk out of a restaurant hand in hand. Their connection and the strong love they have for each other is obvious by their interaction. In my mind I imagine they have been married over fifty years, have several children, grandchildren and great grandchildren to share their lives with. In reality, it might be that it's a third marriage for each of them and she's sleeping around with the guy in the next condo. I refuse to be that cynical. I am forever giving the benefit of the doubt and staying with my romantic version of what the reality tale can look like because I know it exists in the real world.

Some of you will marry again, while the rest of you will remain happily single. The search for the perfect man is over as you learn to focus on yourself and learn to fill in your own empty places. You will begin your own personal odyssey to learn more about who you are and what makes your heart sing. Whatever life choices you make, stay on a path to always improve yourself in mind, body and spirit. When you are on this path, you can totally forget about the whole Prince Charming thing. You will inevitably attract wonderful things and wonderful people into your circle that will add flavor and texture to enhance your life. When and if you are ready, the right guy will find you.

The experience of divorce can be a great teacher. It transforms pain into wisdom and perspective that will help you begin your new life. There is a definite crossroads in divorce where you make a conscious choice to recover or stay wounded; it's as simple as that. The choice you make will be dictated by your attitude and actions. The first step toward recovering starts with forgiveness toward your former spouse, but more important you have to forgive yourself. Beating yourself up and staying in miserable mode for too long gets old, boring and it drains the life out of you. Life is short so make a choice to be happy and make a daily effort to step out of your box and try something different, even if it starts with something simple like taking a new route to work.

Regardless of where you are in the divorce process, you have come a long way. When you are feeling low, remind yourself that you are a princess warrior, an emotional survivor of divorce. Take a few deep breaths and remember that it really is safe to exhale. I'd like to end with two quotes from one of my favorite women in history. I hope her words stay with you and help you when you need that extra little push to move forward into your new life.

You gain strength, courage and confidence
by every experience in which you really stop
to look fear in the face. You are able to say
to yourself, "I have lived through this horror.
I can take the next thing that comes along."
You must do the thing you think you cannot do.

—Eleanor Roosevelt

Healing is a matter of time, but it is
sometimes also a matter of opportunity.

—Eleanor Roosevelt

Epilogue

I had a feeling of hope and adventure, and it was then that I unexpectedly and inconveniently met my real-life Prince Charming. I had a set plan in my head about how my life was going to look over the next few years and having a steady guy a few months after my divorce was not part of my game plan. It certainly didn't involve a man who was twelve years older than me and divorced with four children. I have two children, so with his, we make six! I never liked *The Brady Bunch,* and I always felt men and women should date within their age bracket. The quote "We make plans and God laughs" started to have a lot of meaning for me.

Fortunately, my experience from divorce made me open-minded and less judgmental. I threw caution to the wind and gave this guy a chance. I was planning on dating many different types of guys until I found the one that "fit just right." I resisted falling for him in the beginning and told him I wanted to date other men. Luckily, he was patient and nonjudgmental; he had been divorced and understood my feelings. It wasn't long until I realized just how lucky I was to have found "the guy" right out of the box. It didn't fit my game plan, but here he was, standing right in front of me. I knew from my own experience that this guy was good stuff and he had the qualities and personality I wanted in a mate. I fell in love with a guy that I could really connect with who rocks my world when we kiss. I scrapped my perfect little plan, left the fairy tale behind and started living my "reality tale."

If anybody would have told me my romantic future before my divorce, I would have laughed and said no chance. Turns out all of the "baggage" I was worried about were blessings in disguise. Having been divorced and been in the dating world, my boyfriend became more tuned in to what women want. He also had time to reflect on some of his issues that caused the breakdown in his relationships. His experience and pain forced him to take a better look at himself and become a better man. That old saying that the woman before you paves the way and suffers so he learns to be a better partner in his next relationship just might be true. As far as the age difference, it puts us on even ground most of the time from a maturity standpoint, but his extra years give him wisdom I can learn from.

His children are an unexpected blessing. They are wonderful, partly because they have two amazing parents who share a great friendship as coparents. My boyfriend and his ex have been great role models for how a healthy divorce with children can really work. He has a son and daughter in college and fifteen-year-old twins, a boy and girl. All of the kids are great friends with my children, and they make great babysitters in a pinch. It's great for all of them because they have more people in their lives who love them and want to hang out with them. I have a great relationship with them and feel like the camp counselor. Having two boys is great but it's refreshing to relate to young women and have some more estrogen around.

In all honesty, if they were younger than ten it would be a real challenge and maybe too stressful and hectic. I certainly would not have gone back to changing diapers again. As it is, there are times the whole thing can get messy and complicated. The combination of divorce and children can be a little crazy but worth everything if it's more of the good kind of crazy. I love being in the middle of the high energy chaos when all six of them get together, probably because it doesn't happen that often. I love having alone time with his children so I can enjoy each of their unique personalities. They have also been great teachers when my children come up with issues about divorce. They are a joy and continue to enrich my life as well as my children's.

About the Author

Amy Botwinick is a divorced, single mother of two young boys and makes her home in Boca Raton, Florida, where she is currently enjoying her happily ever after. She has been a chiropractor for the last twelve years and has held a teaching position at a local college. Her business for over a decade has been listening, learning and helping others.

Amy's research and writing convey a directness and honesty that comes from personal experience. To find more resources to help you along your journey of divorce, visit her Web site at *www.todaysdivorced woman.com* or *www.divorcesextoys.com*.